THE DUCK POND AFFAIR ETC

— *Tales From The Cotswolds* —

By the same author

THE BEVIN BOY

ALL OVER THE WOLD

THE DUCK POND AFFAIR ETC

— *Tales From The Cotswolds* —

David Day

SEVEN BOWES-LYON

First published in 2005 by

SEVEN BOWES-LYON
Moreton-in-Marsh
Glos GL56 OEN

Tel 01608 651622
Copyright 2005 © David Day

ISBN: 0-9532454-1-1

Designed and printed by Goodman Baylis Ltd
The Trinity Press, Worcester and London

Contents

1. **THE DUCK POND AFFAIR:**   3
   How a dispute over an ancient pond, half of which belonged to one owner and the other half to another, brought mutiny to Moreton-in-Marsh and mirth to the Nation 1955-57.

2. **ET CETERA:**   33
   A Four Shires Miscellany from the adjoining counties of Gloucester, Oxford, Worcester and Warwick 1954-1984. Including Inter-choral feuding; On the Move with George; Choirmaster to 100,000; Temperamental Mikes; Parable of the Talents; Down at the Front; Summer Resort for Tramps; Death of a Guinea Pig; Guessing the Weight; Master Hornblower; Elusive Church; Innocent Eavesdropper; Thrill of the Auction; The Mickleton Hooter; Room for Reading; the Balloons Came Down; Good Clean Horror; A Lion Escaped; Abnormal Service; Country Calendar; Camp Song; Talk on a Hilltop; Jealousy and Passion; Wisdom Must Pay; Evil Cherub; School with a Grin on its Face; Roast Beef; A Cotswold Monet?; Millennium Eve; Bus Shelter Guest; Gun Totin' Tots; Sunday Refuge and Going Into Hospital.

3. **THE TRIP BACK:**   91
   A fictional story based on a real-life ordeal experienced by some Worcestershire people in the 1950s and 60s.

"Tea up!"

"The great thing, young Fred, is not to let it all go to your 'ead...."

"And who's going the Antarctic and bottle of beer fr

Still Much Binding in the Marsh

By MADELEINE McLOUGHLIN

OH, the binding at Moreton-in-Marsh — all because of the Duck Pond Affair.

The local council said they didn't object to the pond being sold, filled in and turned into a site for garages.

But the locals objected—STRONGLY.

They said the pond added to the beauty of the picturesque High-street in the small Gloucestershire market town (pop. 1,560).

"Skullduggery," some called the plan. And they have won. The duckpond is NOT to be sold.

But the rumpus is far from over.

The townspeople now want to sack the local councillors.

● *Three men in the duck pond rumpus. From the left are council chairman Andrew Horne, councillor Edgar Rolph, and council critic Frank Gardiner.*

Signed by 100

A letter, signed by 100 people, has been sent to the leading figure in the row—Councillor Andrew L. Horne, owner of seven grocery shops and chairman of the council.

It asks him to call a council meeting at which a resolution could be put calling on them to resign.

Mr. Horne told me:

"There is simply no reason why I should explain anything to anyone."

Now a committee of local people, headed by chairman Mr. George Long, a company director, has decided to call a public meeting in a fortnight.

'No Confidence'

Mr. Long said: "A meeting of parishioners passed a vote of no confidence in the council, but seven of the nine members refused to resign."

Mr. Frank Gardiner, 65, a retired gardener, said: "The people are not satisfied with the council. They should go."

Mr. Edgar Rolph, one of the two councillors at loggerheads with the council on the matter, had the last word. He said:

"I think we should accept the verdict of the

● SAYS MRS. IVES OF THE GEORGE & DRAGON INN, WEST WYCOMBE

The George & Dragon Inn, West Wycombe

Dear Sir,
A few months ago my husband and I took over this lovely old coaching inn... I have come to rely on 'Aspro' a good deal because in this new venture colds and 'flu could prove a severe handicap. Quite recently I felt the symptoms of a cold coming on — took 'Aspro' straight away, and checked what might have been the misery of a cold for days...

Yours faithfully,
Pamela Ives

ARM YOURSELF TO FIGHT 'FLU NIGHT AND DAY
Don't ever be caught with a cold, 'flu or a headache, and no 'Aspro'. Get some 'Aspro' today.

+YOU
ND 'FLU
TAKE 'ASPRO'
DY CONQUERS THE GERMS
o' has knocked out the unpleasms that weaken your resistance, seizes the chance to build up its rength to conquer those germs.

mical Double-size Family Pack 3/2

Ladies!
TOPPS
silicone
FURNITURE
means:—
★ NO HARD RUB
★ NO FINGERMA
NO WATERSTAINS
WON'T BLOOM—EVER!

3/6

TOPPS—the amazing Silicone Furniture Cream has already delighted millions of housewives —why not try TOPPS now. You too can have a gleaming home without

The Duck Pond Affair

At Moreton-in-Marsh in Gloucestershire 1955-57

It all began in whispers. People would come up to you in the street, lower their voices and say, "Have you heard? A syndicate is trying to buy up the horse pool," which was what the duck pond was known as in those days. The use of the word "syndicate" was significant because it suggested something powerful, furtive and anonymous, and practically every businessman of substance in the town was alleged to belong to this syndicate at some time or other. That they should be interested in acquiring such a scruffy local landmark as the horse pool and be so secretive about it made everyone suspicious. What was the syndicate up to? Was this the first move in a campaign to take over the town by stealth? And it was this feeling that something underhand was going on and a determination to frustrate it that characterised the duck pond affair from beginning to end. Hardly anyone cared about the pond itself, which had been an unloved eyesore for years.

Moreton-in-Marsh is a small Cotswold town situated in Gloucestershire close to its borders with the counties of Oxford, Warwick and Worcester. A classical pillar a mile away marks the spot where the counties converged for centuries and is known as the Four Shires Stone. It has been argued that the town got its distinctive name because of its situation adjacent to these boundaries: in other words, it was "in March" or borderland, but this has since been discounted. The name means exactly what it says: the area, which is flat and open, was also damp at one time with the town referred to as Moreton Henmarsh, which accounts for the "in-Marsh" rather than the "in-the-Marsh" that many people prefer to use.

The town also stands at the intersection of two main traffic routes, the east-west Oxford to Worcester road leading eventually to mid-Wales, and the north-south Fosse Way from Lincoln to Exeter and the West Country, originally built by the Romans, whose foundation stones still lie under High Street. In the mid-1950s the population stood at about 1,900, which modest size caused some tactless visitors to refer to Moreton-in-Marsh as a village yet it never looked anything other than a town with a long broad main street-cum-market place with raised pavements on either side, presided over by a bulky 19th century town hall, almost opposite the offices of the North Cotswold District Council, which administered the area and had its headquarters here; and just around the corner was the railway station with a staff of 20 serving the main line from Paddington to the cathedral cities of Worcester and Hereford. All this coming and going made Moreton-in-Marsh more extrovert and accessible than most Cotswold towns at that time. There were always plenty of outsiders to be seen in transit.

Unlike the other places, however, the town is not prized for its architecture or beauty. Cotswold stone predominates, of course, but there is a sufficient intrusion of red brick and Welsh slate to irritate the purist, and yet the High Street curves pleasantly on its western side, trees abound and the buildings, which include several banks and old coaching inns, form an harmonious ensemble. The Victorian church hides itself in a side street and after the town hall, the most conspicuous structure is the 17th century curfew tower, where the bell was rung until 1860 when the town was deemed orderly enough to manage without it. The Lord Chancellor, Viscount Sankey, who was born in Moreton-in-Marsh in 1866, once said of his birthplace, "Century after century everything here has been unhurried, quiet and orderly," but he died seven years before the duck pond affair erupted, otherwise he might have felt differently.

The horse pool, later to become the duck pond, lies at the southern end of High Street, next to the Fosse Way, and it was certainly no credit to the town in those austerity years after the Second World War. For much of the time it was half empty, revealing a bed of dried mud and weeds littered with old cans, and during the winter it flooded over the road. Opinion was divided about just what sort of pond it was. Some said it was merely a sump dug there by wise old countrymen many years ago to take excess surface water during periods of heavy rain. Others maintained it was a genuine pond fed by an underground spring.

Whatever the explanation, this dirty old pond, roughly 60 metres long by 20 wide or 195 feet by 65, certainly had one feature that made it unique: it was divided in two. One half of the water belonged to one owner, the other half to another. For at least 100 years the half nearest the road had belonged to the parish, the present custodians being the Parish Council. The other half went with University Farm, whose venerable farmhouse stood in nearby High Street with the date 1678 engraved on its walls. And it was in 1955 when parts of University Farm came up for sale in various lots, including the western half of the horse pool, that the duck pond saga truly began.

At their meeting on February 17 of that year the Parish Council were intrigued to get a letter from John Drury, of Sheldon Bosley's, the local estate agents and auctioneers, saying that a client of his was interested in buying the pond and asking whether the council would be willing to sell whatever part of it belonged to them, The council, thinking they might be on to a good thing here, decided to reply that they were quite prepared to sell provided the pool was to be made proper use of.

At their next meeting in March the council received a reply from Mr Drury saying that he had consulted his client who, subject to planning permission being given and technical advice being satisfactory, proposed to drain the pond, divert any spring water and develop the site for building lock-up garages for which it was thought there would be a good demand. The proposal was subject to his client being able to purchase the remainder of the pond and it was hoped the council would be prepared to sell their half for a nominal sum.

The Parish Council consisted of nine members: Andrew Horne, the chairman' Gerald Clifton, the vice-chairman, and the brothers Ernest and Edgar Rolph, Bill Tarplett, Reg Drury, Alan Heeks, Fred Arthurs and Arthur Saxton. Only one woman, a schoolteacher, had been elected during the 60 years since parish councils were formed and she had quickly come and gone, enabling the all-male club to resume its monopoly of power as before. Mr Clifton and Mr Drury were both butchers, Mr Tarplett, a farmer, Mr Heeks, a milk roundsman, and Dr Saxton, one of the town's three medical practitioners. The others, with the exception of the chairman, were either retired or semi-retired.

Mr Horne, who was to play a major role in the duck pond affair, was the owner of a wholesale grocers' in Moreton-in-Marsh and a chain of other stores throughout the North Cotswolds, a family business going back 150 years. Aged just over 50, he was a tallish, silver-haired, dignified man with an urbane manner and adroit way of conducting meetings, and oozed integrity. One sensed that he felt a genuine commitment both to his business and the town generally and was determined to serve both to the best of his ability. If he had a fault it was that he viewed the council's transactions through a businessman's unsentimental profit-and-loss eye. He would certainly have regarded half a horse pool as a liability that the council would do well to get rid of if the price were right.

The outcome of that March meeting was that the council decided to inform Mr Drury that they were willing to proceed with negotiations for the sale of the pond but would take no further action until they had heard that his client, whom we shall have to refer to as "Mr X" for the time being, had been successful in obtaining the other half of the pond. "Mr X" subsequently bought that half but continued to maintain his anonymity, thus exacerbating local gossip which became more and more convinced that something funny was going on. The District Valuer set a price of £10 on the council's half of the pond.

At the council's meeting on October 20, 1955, Mr Drury wrote that his client accepted the asking price of £10 for their half and requested permission to go in and drain the pond. The council met monthly in the offices of their clerk, John Barkes, a solicitor in a practice founded by his late father, who had been Parish Council clerk before him: indeed, father and son had been the only persons ever to hold this office in Moreton-in-Marsh. You entered their front door in leafy Oxford Street, went up the stairs to a landing and turned a doorknob and stepped into Mr Barkes's sanctum, which was piled high almost from floor to ceiling with legal volumes, security boxes with individuals' names painted on them and deeds and other documents tied up with pink tape.

These meetings may have saved the ratepayers money by avoiding the need to hire a room but technically they were quite illegal because a council must meet in a place to which the public has access and once I, the newspaper reporter, had squeezed in, there was not an inch of space left for any other observer. One of the after effects of the duck pond affair was that this practice had to stop and the council subsequently met in rented accommodation where there was enough room for the public to attend as spectators if they wished.

A solicitor of the old school, usually dressed in a black morning suit and with a turn of speech including many an "emerging therefrom" or "arising thereout", Mr Barkes was a courteous, self effacing and above all things, cautious gentleman. He advised the council that they could not possibly allow Mr Drury's client to have access to the pond at this stage. For one thing they still had to get the consent of a parish meeting before they could dispose of the pond. The council agreed though Edgar Rolph pointed out that the client might just as well go ahead with draining his half because it was the only part with any water in it at present.

Significantly it was Mr Rolph, later to turn rebel, who successfully moved that the council obtain the consent of a parish meeting as quickly as possible. He and his brother, middle-aged to elderly members of an old local family, were to become staunch defenders of the horse pool later on though otherwise they had little in common. Ernest, the elder, was tall, thin, softly spoken, a magistrate and very much a man of peace. Edgar was stocky, rubicund and belligerent, thrived on controversy and loved nothing better than a good verbal dust-up.

Another councillor to play an important role was Dr Saxton, a droll, boyish character in his thirties with dark horn-rimmed specs and a vivacity of manner and speech that did much to brighten council meetings. He said the present condition of the horse pool was "absolutely revolting" with the exposed portions littered with empty petrol cans, and the council agreed to pay someone to remove them.

The clerk had unknowingly put his finger on a fatal weakness in the council's case when he mentioned that they had to get the consent of a parish meeting to dispose of their half of the pond. Those living in large towns miss a great deal by having no parish meetings to go to. At least one such meeting must be held each Spring. At one time it had to be in March but the period was later extended to include April and May, and on this particular evening the local council tend to find themselves pushed into the background by their electors, who normally have to hold their discussions in bars, women's groups or over the family hearth. Little wonder that councillors blench when Spring and the annual reckoning draws near, especially it they happen to glance at the minute book and see a host of things they had promised to do last year and had since lamentably left undone.

Not that a council have to obey a parish meeting. They can take an entirely different course if they want to though obviously they cannot fail to be influenced by what a parish meeting says. In only one respect must they do what a parish-meeting tells them and that is when it comes to disposing of parish property, and this, of course, was where Moreton-in-Marsh Parish Council came unstuck. Badly unstuck! Perhaps the council had become complacent. Few electors showed any interest in local government in the town. No-one attended the council's monthly meeting to see what went on - not that he could have got into the room anyway! And the annual parish meeting was feebly supported and all over in a few minutes as a rule. Other parishes might have their rows but at Moreton-in-Marsh everything went serenely. Until the duck pond affair, that is!

A parish meeting was convened in the hall at the back of the Congregational chapel on Monday, November 30, and despite all the talk in the town, was attended by less than 20 people, though this may have been due to it being inadequately advertised: just one sheet of printed foolscap in the window of a private house and another in a glass-fronted noticeboard outside the district council offices that no-one ever looked at. The Congregational Hall was where the council usually held parish meetings: not too big, not too small and with Biblical pictures and texts on the walls for inspiration and the odd memorial plaque here or there to remind us of time passing and our own mortality.

Mr Horne, in the chair, began by saying that for a long time the council had been concerned about the untidy state of the horse pool. It was used by people as a rubbish tip and the council incurred expense in having to have it cleaned out. They had now received an offer for their half of the pond from the owner of the other half who was willing to pay £10 for it, the price fixed by the District Valuer. The council had agreed to the sale but must first obtain the consent of a parish meeting.

All seemed set for a quick decision and an early sale.

But by this time the horse pool had found a formidable ally and "Mr X" a rival who was sufficiently well-off to match him pound for pound. Some years before there had been a nice little teacher at St David's Junior C of E School in the town, called Miss Cynthia Parsons, a quiet, unremarkable young woman who had left the school to get married. She had now returned a very different person, a poised, attractive and obviously well-to-do widow, Mrs Hooley by name, who had bought some old cottages in Church Street and converted them into a beautiful home, which she had called Basil Tree Cottage, and she was very much in favour of keeping the horse pool as it was. What is more important, she was present at the meeting.

She declared. "If the site is going to be used as a means of income, wouldn't it be better for the council to put their half on the open market? I would be quite happy to buy your half and keep it as a pond. I have never taken part in a parish meeting before and haven't any idea who the owner of the other half is, but he will be getting a very good site from the council for practically nothing and can then use it for his own purposes.

"I like Moreton-in-Marsh as it is - that's why I came back to live here. I would like to see the horse pool kept the same with trees round, even with weeds growing in it. I don't think a block of garages would be at all suitable for that site."

Dr Saxton responded with alacrity, as was his wont, explaining, "We only have half of the pond. If we had the whole pond I would like to see a duck pond, too, but I can't see what good half a duck pond is to anyone. The council ought to have tried for the other half when it came up for auction but we didn't and the only thing we can do now is to sell our half."

It was the first time the horse pool had been publicly referred to as a duck pond.

The chairman then proposed and Reg Drury seconded, that the council sell their half to the owner of the other half, but Edgar Rolph, who had obviously been listening to the muttering in the town and was now shifting his position somewhat, said that in order to test the feeling of the meeting he would propose an amendment that the council sell their half by public auction or tender, and Mrs Hooley seconded. By proposing an amendment to a motion that the council, including himself, had unanimously approved beforehand, Mr Rolph was committing an awful breach of local government etiquette. It is customary for a council to stand united in such circumstances and the consequences on this occasion were to prove devastating.

When the amendment was put to the meeting, it was carried by eight votes to seven.

The result clearly nettled Mr Horne, not so much because the decision had gone against him but because it had been brought about by councillors actually voting against their own proposition, an unprecedented folly, and he did something that a chairman rarely feels impelled to do. First, he used his personal vote to make the result eight-eight and then his casting vote, as chairman, to defeat the amendment by nine votes to eight. Not that this manoeuvre did him any good because when the original motion to sell was put to the meeting it was defeated by 10 votes to seven, and for the first time Mr Horne's smooth facade crumbled. "I do not wish to question the intelligence of the parish meeting," he said tartly, "but I feel that in this matter they have acted very foolishly. There is no escaping the fact that the part of the pond belonging to the council is nothing but a liability."

And there the parish meeting ended but the fun had only just begun!

In the issue of the Cotswold Journal dated December 12, 1955, the week after my report of the parish meeting had appeared, there were two letters on the subject of the horse pool, the first from Eric Rolph, a poultry farmer and nephew of councillors Ernest and Edgar Rolph. "In these days of universal concern with such fearful things as nuclear bombs it is indeed refreshing to see that such trivia as the future of the local duck pond can excite such interest," he wrote. "One gathers from your account of the recent parish meeting that there is no such thing as apathy in local government when it is a question of the disposal of the parish council's liquid assets. One is impressed, too, by the way the business was conducted, particularly the chairman's notable restraint in not wishing to question the intelligence of the meeting. Such old world courtesy is becoming rare."

The other letter came from Arthur Martin, a newcomer to Moreton-in-Marsh, who lived over the Post Office, where he worked. "May I say that the pond has for some considerable time been an offence to the eye, a danger to the health of the community and a danger to our children," he said. "On warm weather the pond almost dries up, revealing tin cans, stones, old iron and other rubbish. The smell then arising ought long ago to have been piped direct to sittings of the parish council with the object of stirring some of the members to action in the name of hygiene. In wintertime, when frozen over, half of the children in the district have to be restrained from skating there, while the other half arrive home wet and cold after making the attempt. It may be said that my opinions ought to have been expressed at the parish meeting. I would gladly have done so had I not, in common with 90 per cent of the parishioners, been unaware that a meeting was being held."

When parish councillors turned up for their next monthly meeting on December 19, they were no doubt expecting a right ticking of from their chairman and got one. "When the council decided to sell their half of the pond no-one voted against it and to the best of my knowledge nobody has ever been opposed to it," Mr Horne said. "I mention this because as chairman of the parish meeting I found myself in an exceedingly invidious position. Not a single member of this council spoke in support of the proposal and an amendment was proposed by a member of the council and the original proposition defeated as a result of the voting of the parish council. We went as a united body to get something done and we ourselves defeated it."

Edgar Rolph, the only one with the face to reply, said the secrecy which had surrounded the proposed sale had made the parish suspicious. "I proposed an amendment to show the council was not ashamed to put up the pond for public auction or tender," he said.

The big surprise of the meeting, however, was that "Mr X" chose this moment to reveal his identity by writing personally to the council and what a revelation it proved to be! It was none other than Major John David Summers, of Little Barrow, a Cotswold mansion just outside the town, one of the wealthiest men in the district and the last person in the world one would expect to find owning half a horse pool.

An old Etonian and ex-Guards officer, he moved to the Cotswolds soon after the war and became active in farming and local government, serving as a member of the North Cotswold District Council (of which he was eventually chairman), Gloucestershire County Council and the county branch of the National Farmers' Union for whom he became a London delegate. A tall man in his thirties with thick, straight, dark brown hair that used to flop over his forehead, he was married with a young family and though well-intentioned had a tendency to put his foot in it, as, for example, with the duck pond. His was the only name to be publicly linked with the pond and all the talk of a syndicate appears to have been ill-founded though it was a long time before the town felt able to shed its suspicions. Nor did it ever become quite clear how such a distinguished local figure as the Major came to be involved in plans to build lock-up garages on the site of a horse pool.

"I think it is only right that I should publicly declare that I am the owner of the western half of Moreton-in-Marsh horse pool," Major Summers wrote," and that Sheldon Bosley has been acting on my behalf for the purchase of the eastern half. I assure you and the whole parish that I intend to commit no architectural monstrosity at the approach to the town from the south... My original proposal was to build a swimming pool here but I am advised the cost will be too great. I, therefore, intend to build on the site of the pond an office building in Cotswold stone together with lock-up garages behind. I believe there is a growing need for garages in the town and I believe these should be provided by private enterprise and not by the district council. I, therefore, hope you will allow this matter to be raised at a further parish meeting and that the parish will allow me to purchase the other half of the horse pool, which I propose to develop for the benefit of the inhabitants of Moreton-in-Marsh."

If parish councillors were sceptical of Major Summers' original proposal to build a swimming pool, as they might well have been, they did not show it. It was - and always had been - the wish of Moretonians to have their own swimming pool and the letter certainly touched a nerve in this respect but it was hard to believe that the horse pool could have provided a suitable site for such a project.

Major Summers's rival, Mrs Hooley, was not to be caught napping and she had sent a letter too. "I am willing to give up to £50 towards the expense of putting the parish's half of the horse pond in good order," she said. "I am also willing to contribute £10 per annum while I live here to maintain it in good order. The pond will then be an amenity and no longer a source of worry to the parish."

These two letters put the council in a dilemma. Major Summers's offer would enable them to get rid of their unwanted half of the pond but they hesitated to reject Mrs Hooley's offer out of hand, bearing in mind how the parish felt or was beginning to feel about keeping the pond. But if they accepted her money what good would it do them when they only owned half the pond?

As usual Dr Saxton came galloping to the rescue by successfully moving that the council call another parish meeting to ask permission to sell their half of the pond to Major Summers. If he had left it there all might have been well but, unfortunately, he did not. He impulsively added, "If we do not get that vote then I think we should all resign. This thing has caused a great deal of talk in the town and now is the time to see whether we have got the confidence of the parish. We have got to be democratic about this."

These remarks were to prove embarrassing for all concerned later on.

When the motion to accept Major Summers's offer of £10 was put to the meeting, only Ernest and Edgar Rolph voted against. Edgar proposed that the council accept Mrs Hooley's offer and Ernest seconded, but this was defeated, and it was decided to hold a second parish meeting in the Congregational Hall on Monday, January 9, 1956. Dr Saxton, who seemed determined to put the noose round the council's neck, asked, "If we are beaten, shall we resign?"

Mr Horne said, "If the majority of councillors wish to make this a matter of confidence in the parish council I am prepared to stand by them," but the clerk, Mr Barkes, never one to stick his own or anyone else's neck out, interposed, "I think it would be exceedingly unwise"' and how right he proved to be.

As the day of the meeting drew near it became obvious that feelings in the town were running so high that the moderately large Congregational Hall might not prove big enough to take the number of parishioners wanting to attend and at the last minute there was a more expensive change of venue to the spacious town hall, the noble pile occupying the centre of High Street. It was a wise move because eventually no less than 200 people crammed into the hall, making it the biggest parish meeting ever to have taken place not only in Moreton-in-Marsh but in the whole of the North Cotswolds.

More properly known as the Redesdale Hall, the building dates from 1887, Queen Victoria's golden jubilee year, and commemorates John Thomas Freeman-Mitford, the first and last Earl Redesdale, a bachelor, who died at Batsford Park, Moreton-in-Marsh's great house, in 1886, leaving a fortune to his cousin, Algernon Bertram Freeman-Mitford, who was so overcome that he built the hall and planted a grand avenue of lime trees in High Street to go with it, in honour of his benefactor.

The hall was designed by the London architect, Sir Ernest George, and drew its inspiration from the ancient guild or market halls raised on open arches, its outstanding feature being an oaken clock tower, 76 feet high to the top of its gold boars head's weather vane. Inside it has a church-like timber-vaulted roof, panelled walls and stained glass windows bearing heraldic designs associated with the Mitfords who originate from the Redesdale area of Northumbria. The building cost Mr Mitford £10,000 but undeterred he went on to spend even more on remodelling Batsford Park and its gardens, employing, it is said, 200 men for six months.

He, himself, was ennobled as the 1st Baron Redesdale in 1905 after entertaining his friend, Kind Edward VII, at Moreton-in-Marsh, and was later to become grandfather of the fascinating Mitford girls, several of whom were born at Batsford Park though by this time the family's wealth was not what it had been and they had to move to less grandiose quarters elsewhere.

In 1950 the hall was presented to the North Cotswold District Council who accepted in haste and repented at leisure because the building proved a dreadful white elephant, expensive to maintain and with such inadequate lavatories that desperate males at Saturday night dances felt obliged to seek relief in the street outside where the local Constabulary was ready and waiting to apprehend them and cart them off to the Petty Sessions, whose coffers swelled with the fines the hapless offenders had to pay for their incontinence.

The hall was also the devil to keep warm: not that this was a problem on the night of the parish meeting with so many bodies packed within and so much heat, both physical and metaphorical, being generated. Even the stuffed animal heads, big game trophies recently donated to the hall, hanging lugubriously on the walls above, seemed to be showing signs of animation. Mr Horne, the only standing figure on the platform, looked very vulnerable facing such a tight militant throng.

He explained that the council had already sought permission from a previous parish meeting to sell their half of the pond but their proposal had been turned down by 10 voters. They felt that such a decision should not be made by such a small number and had decided to call another parish meeting, and he proposed the council sell their half for £10 and Mr Clifton, the vice-chairman, seconded.

There was a huge approving roar when Abe Howe, a bricklayer, got up and said, "What I should like to know, Mr Chairman, is whether you have a finger in the pie in this matter. It seems there has been something underhanded going on and I shall propose that the entire parish council be asked to resign their seats."

As the cheering died down, Mr Horne, who was to have a most uncomfortable evening but who never lost his composure no matter what the provocation, replied, "As far as those remarks concern me personally I shall be quite prepared to answer them privately after the meeting. As far as your proposition is concerned, we already have one proposition before the meeting and I am not in a position to receive another until that one has been dealt with."

Arthur Martin, one of the correspondents to the Cotswold Journal, bravely decided to say a good word for the council. "If the proposal is carried, the purchaser will develop the property and pay rates on it from which the entire parish will benefit," he said.

His remarks prompted the classic retort from an entrenched countryman when confronted with someone whom he regards as an interfering outsider. "What do you know about it, gaffer?" came a loud voice from the back of the hall. "You ain't been in the place five minutes'"

More xenophobia came from Mrs Alice Warmington who said an offer had been made by Mrs Hooley to buy the council's half of the pond for more than Major Summers. "Why haven't they accepted this offer?" she said. "I would rather see someone in Moreton-in-Marsh have it than an outsider". More cheering ensued.

The meeting then took a surreal turn when two live ducks were tossed in the air from somewhere in the hall and sent flapping and quacking over the heads of the assembly towards the platform to the cry of: "Let's have some of these on the pond again" The old name of the horse pool died at that instant: henceforward it was to be the duck pond for evermore.

"We are all indebted to the gentleman who has enlivened these proceedings with ducks," said Mr Horne calmly. "Might I on behalf of the serious-minded people present, ask him to remove them or keep them under proper control."

After the birds had been recaptured, Eric Rolph, the other correspondent to the Cotswold Journal, also spoke. "I don't think many people really care whether the pond is filled in or kept as it is," he said. "The whole point of this business is the furtive manner in which this sale has been engineered. Major Summers did not come into the open until a parish meeting had turned his offer down. The Parish Council were elected to conserve the interests of the parish and to guard its property yet they were prepared to sell their half of the pond to an unknown buyer for an unknown purpose and for a miserable sum. They are not safe to be trusted with any further parish property!"

All this proved too much for Dr Saxton who felt impelled to retaliate. "I think we are missing the whole point of this meeting," he said. "We do not own the duck pond. We only own half of it and the ratepayers have such a high regard for the pond that they chuck all their empty tins in it. I ought to know because I've fished 27 petrol tins out of it myself. Do you really want the pond to stay as it is - all that black water, black mud and old bricks? Let's be serious about this! I'm delighted that feeling is high over this duck pond but I am sorry that a rather nasty feeling has got into the debate to the effect that members of the council are getting something out of this. That's a damn lie!"

When the motion to sell was put to the meeting it was massively defeated by 132 votes to 59 but the proceedings did not end there. A further sensation lay in store. After the vote had been taken Stanley Wass, a Moreton-in-Marsh hardware merchant and builder, asked for and was given permission to read a letter which, he said, had been given him by Major Summers earlier in the evening to read to the meeting. Mr Wass had a problem with his aitches with the result that his references to Major Summers's property tended to come out as "'is 'alf of the 'orse pool", a solecism that if anything seemed to confirm his reputation as a blunt-spoken, no nonsense sort of bloke though his words were less well received than usual on this occasion. The letter began: "As someone who dislikes strife and has no desire at all to split the parish regarding the retention or otherwise of the horse pool, I have tonight decided to withdraw my offer for the half of the pool belonging to the parish..."

There was such an outburst of vociferous booing and jeering at this point that Mr Wass was unable to make himself heard, with or without aspirates, and had to stop reading and sit down. The meeting obviously felt that he had been waiting to see which way the voting went before reading the letter and that if it had gone the other way, the letter might never have been read at all.

At last the noise subsided and he continued:... "and to offer to the parish council my half of the horse pool on condition that the council pay me the sum of money I paid for my half of £10 and my expenses to date and that permanent arrangements are made for the proper upkeep of the whole horse pool by the parish council. I am sure this action is the correct one and should leave all content with no bitterness. It is then up to the council to take whatever decision the parish requires them to take for the future of the pool. I am taking this action because I sincerely believe that unity in a small country town is of vital importance and I hope my action tonight will help towards that desirable end."

The Duck Pond Affair

There was irony in Mr Horne's voice as he said, "I must thank Mr Wass for holding back this letter until the end so as not to spoil our evening's enjoyment," and he then closed the meeting leaving the council defeated yet again with half an unwanted duck pond on their hands. The question now was whether they were going to resign

The news from Moreton-in-Marsh had been attracting considerable attention in both the regional and national newspapers and on radio and television, then in its black-and-white infancy. People everywhere seemed fascinated by a town with a divided duck pond and its inhabitants' struggle to prevent the pond from being sold and filled in, and when the story broke about live ducks having been let loose at the meeting there were excited headlines and broadcasts not only in this country but abroad. The ducks had been smuggled into the hall by John Rolph, Ernest's son, and his bride-to-be, Pat Trice, having been borrowed from a farm in the neighbouring village of Todenham. As a result of their action the young couple achieved more than just local fame and were interviewed by newspapers and filmed for television. Even the ducks had their photographs taken!

"The Times" wrote a donnish article about the pond and the London "Evening Standard" went completely over the top with an editorial which said, "As always, vain and contemptuous authority has failed to reckon with the ardour of free men roused in defence of their heritage. Eyesore the council might call the duck pond but before the village would part with their half of it, they would see the structure of local government lie in ruins!"

The comedian, Richard Murdoch, who was appearing in one of the most popular programmes on British radio, called "Much Binding In The Marsh", came down to interview customers at the White Horse, the pub next to the duck pond, and this prompted an evening newspaper to print a poem to be sung to the programme's signature tune, the first verse going:

At Much Binding In The Marsh
There used to be a horse pool, I remember;
At Much Binding In The Marsh
It changed its name to duck pond last December.

The Parish Council want to sell it to a Major S:
The parish says, "Oh no you don't, we're sticking to that mess'
And ever since that day it's made big headlines in the Press
At Much Binding In The Marsh!

A news film about the pond for national distribution was shown at Moreton-in-Marsh's cinema, The Playhouse, and a series of anonymous cartoons began to appear on noticeboards drawn by someone with a satiric bent. Soon Moretonians began to get letters and Press cuttings from relatives and friends in other parts of the country and all over the world regarding the duck pond affair, asking what on earth was going on. Meanwhile the nation was holding its breath to see whether the Parish Council was going to do the so-called honourable thing and resign.

The next meeting of the council on January 19, 1956, was held in the Congregational Hall instead of the clerk's office to accommodate the large number of local government electors wishing to attend as spectators. Mr Horne said he was pleased to see so many present. It was the first time in his recollection that any member of the public had attended a council meeting.

The question of resignation was immediately raised by Edgar Rolph who said, "We as a council asked for a vote of confidence which was strongly rejected and I think that as honourable men we should accept the verdict of the majority of parishioners and resign as parish councillors. I make a proposition to that effect."

"It is not my custom to interfere with a proposition," replied Mr Horne, "but I really am compelled to point out that yours is based on a fallacy. The seconder of the resolution put to the parish meeting will bear me out that it was worded with the greatest care to avoid making the resignation of this council automatic on an adverse decision by the meeting."

The rest of the council supported this view, apart from the Rolph brothers, and that, for the time being, proved to be that. The council had no intention of resigning.

The next development was a meeting at one of the old coaching inns, the Redesdale Arms Hotel, on Friday, January 21, attended by 36 electors, who unanimously sent the following letter to the council: "As you are no doubt aware a fairly large section of the parishioners are very dissatisfied with the Parish Council over the manner in which they have acted over the proposed sale of the horse pool. This feeling of mistrust has been evident all through the proceedings and was very forcibly expressed at the parish meeting. The council's proposal to dispose of the property was so worded as to convey to the majority of parishioners that it should be taken as a vote of confidence in the council and the subsequent action of the council in refusing to resign after being so overwhelmingly defeated may have disgusted some and disappointed others but most certainly destroyed what little respect the parishioners might have had for the Parish Council.

"It is the opinion of a good many parishioners that they should be given an early opportunity to officially record their feelings in this matter and it is therefore on their behalf that we respectfully request you to convene a parish meeting in accordance with statutory regulations in order that the following resolution may be placed before the assembly: 'That we, the parishioners, have no confidence in the present Parish Council and request their resignation'."

Not unnaturally the council declined to call yet another parish meeting, the sole purpose of which was to make them resign, and so one had to be called by the statutory number of six local government electors and this took place in the Redesdale Hall on Monday, February 20, 1956.

By the time Winter had the Cotswolds firmly in its grip. Snow covered the uplands, temperatures fell below freezing and ice crunched underfoot as citizens trudged their way to yet another parish meeting. The Cotswold winters are harsh and memories went back to the awesome winter of 1947, only nine years before, when Moreton-in-Marsh had been the coldest place in Great Britain, an experience that no-one in the town wanted to go through again. Yet despite the bitter cold and the temptation to stay at home, over 100 people attended the meeting at which a retired Naval officer, Lieutenant-commander Thomas Clarke-Irons, who was an elector, was duly appointed to preside.

The national status acquired by the duck pond affair was well illustrated by a point made by George Long, manager of the local engineering works, when he said, "The Government are holding a debate at the moment on which there is a vote of confidence. If we let our parish council get away with it, this will be setting a precedent for the Government." In other words, what Moreton-in-Marsh does today, Westminster may do tomorrow!

When the motion of no confidence in the council was put to the meeting, 55 voted in favour and two against, and the resolution was handed to Mr Horne the next morning, the day of the council's usual monthly meeting.

At this meeting Major Summers, who was present, said he wanted £10 for his half of the pond together with £39 compensation for money spent on drainage.

Mrs Hooley wrote that she was prepared to pay the £10 but nothing for the drainage which had been done prematurely in preparation for filling in the pond and was, in her opinion, illegal.

As so often happens when councils find themselves in an awkward situation, the meeting agreed to put off the evil day by deferring until their next meeting on Tuesday, March 20, their decision on whether to resign and whether to buy the other half of the pond. Edgar Rolph could not wait that long and sent in his resignation forthwith, probably the best thing for him to do because he was now totally aligned with the anti-council faction. The question remained as to whether the rest of the council would follow his example.

Readers will have noticed that over half of those present at the special parish meeting on February 20 had abstained when it came to voting against the council and this indicated a softening of local opinion. Many felt that the duck pond had been saved and that to continue to harry the council was merely being vindictive.

The Cotswold Journal wrote, "To prolong the controversy, especially when so much of the good humour has gone out of it, seems ill-advised. After receiving such a buffeting over their proposal to sell the pond, the council deserve an opportunity to redeem themselves. Events have taught them that while a government can dispose of an Empire, a parish council, being closer to the people, cannot dispose of half a duck pond so easily. And having learnt this important lesson perhaps they will be good little boys in future."

A letter to the Cotswold Journal, dated February 23, from a Moreton-in-Marsh undergraduate, David Currill, of Pembroke College, Oxford, made a similar point. "Dazzled by the publicity on radio, television and films and in newspapers, the people of Moreton-in-Marsh seem to have forgotten that the original cause of contention, the duck pond, has been settled," he said. 'The situation now appears to be one of personal animosity between certain members of the council, some of whom are seeking local support. Before taking what can only be rash steps to force the council to resign, the people would do well to consider the great amount of work done by the members of the council and how difficult it would be to replace them adequately. Surely this is more important than what is becoming distasteful publicity?"

The duck pond saga reached its climax during the third week of March 1956 when by coincidence the annual parish meeting was due to take place on Monday the 19th and the monthly council meeting the following evening. Once again the parish meeting, the fourth in less than four months, was held in the Redesdale Hall when 130 people turned up to see what was going to happen to the pond and whether the council were going to resign.

Mr Horne's usual practice when conducting a meeting was to keep quiet and let everyone talk themselves into a tangle, then make a suggestion which would be gratefully accepted and which was exactly what he had wanted in the first place. On this occasion, however, he reversed his usual tactics and came out with all guns firing. "After receiving such a clear and unmistakable rebuttal to their proposal to sell the duck pond, the council accepted without question the desire of the parish to retain its half of the pond," he said. "That, one would have thought, would have been the end of the matter but proved, in fact, to be the beginning of a campaign starting with private meetings, fostered by local, regional and national publicity culminating in a parish meeting at which a resolution calling upon the council to resign was passed.

"Much could be said about this campaign: the alacrity with which the only parish councillor involved aligned himself with what promised in his eyes to be the winning side; the eager welcome given to publicity of all sorts; the very biased views expressed in such publicity; the success of the campaign in turning the parish into an object of ridicule in the eyes of the country; the many base insinuations and suggestions of malpractice made against members of the council. We do not propose to reply to them in detail. Tempting as it may be to retaliate in kind we prefer to rely upon the record and reputations of the council, all of whom have served the public faithfully and most of them for many years...

"Why then should the parish council resign? Because we are told 50 odd local government electors of this parish have no confidence in us. We know that 300 or 400 electors had sufficient confidence to vote us into office a year ago and they have shown no sign that they have changed their minds. The council maintain they have served the parish faithfully during their term of office and they consider it their duty to complete the term of their appointment and they intend to do so."

If this speech were intended to flatten the opposition from the outset it certainly succeeded. Eric Rolph said publicity had not been sought. Newspapers had taken up the matter of their own accord. Miss Hilda Drucker said it was nonsense to say that a paper like "The Times" would have become involved for petty spiteful reasons. But the opposition had been routed and knew it and was on the retreat though a lively parting shot came from one of its leaders, Commander Clarke-Irons, who said, "We should applaud the decision of the parish council because they are so sure in their own minds of their own integrity and we should thank them for their services to the community because it is very likely that after the next election they will not be there to represent us'"

At their usual meeting the next evening the council decided that they were not only not going to resign but they were not going to buy Major Summers's half of the pond either, which meant that the saga had returned right back to where it started with one half belonging to the parish and the other, to a private owner!

Ernest Rolph wrote saying he felt it his duty to tender his resignation and his letter was received with much regret, He had been a member of the council for many years and was a far less contentious person than his buccaneering younger brother. After noting the feelings of the parish, the Rolph family had consistently opposed the sale of the pond and were as much as anyone responsible for seeing that this old, albeit disreputable-looking feature of the town was preserved.

As the winter's snow dissolved into Spring Mr Mitford's lime trees in High Street burst into new leaf, the lilacs in the road to the station blossomed to welcome travellers, the damp meadows by the railway track shone with marsh marigolds while on the other side of town the hedgerows in the Landgate fields exhaled the perfume of hawthorn in bloom. By June the Civil Defence volunteers were at it again, trying their hand at emergency cooking with makeshift outdoor ovens in preparation for what they might have to do if a Third World War were to occur as was half-feared with the Soviet Union armed, hostile and suspicious behind its Iron Curtain.

Recruiting for Civil Defence had gone well in the North Cotswolds unlike some other parts of the country where the pessimists regarded it as unlikely to do any good in the face of a nuclear war, and regular exercises were held with special effects provided by thunderflashes, magnesium flares and smoke candles. But it was at emergency cooking that the volunteers excelled, their masterwork having been a stew consisting of two cwt of potatoes, half cwt of carrots, 75lbs of beef, 28 lbs of onions and 10 lbs of flour, fed to American Servicemen without significant damage to Anglo-US relations.

This time the challenge was to provide a midday meal for everyone at Moreton-in-Marsh Cottage Hospital and after setting up an emergency kitchen at the rear of the institution on the morning of June 5, 1956, the volunteers succeeded in producing the inevitable stew followed by jam tart and custard for the staff and their patients, who were certainly no worse after the experience than they had been before.

With the coming of Summer the council must have enjoyed a measure of satisfaction on beholding the appearance of the duck pond which dried up as usual and became a repellent mudhole. One could almost hear them crowing, "All right! You wanted to save the pond! Well now you've got it! And just look at it! Doesn't it make you feel proud?" It was true, of course. The pond had been saved but neither the parish council nor the private owner, who had both come

The Duck Pond Affair Etc.

to grief as a result of it, were prepared to waste any more of their time or money on it. And so the pond just got shabbier and shabbier.

By late August the uplands were golden brown with ripe corn and it was time for the members of the Moreton-in-Marsh and District Agricultural and Horse Show Society to go on their annual tour of the champion crops, which ended up at the home - or more likely the garden - of their current president, whose hospitality called to mind the alfresco harvest gatherings of yore except that sherry and canapes were more likely to be served than cider and hunks of bread and cheese. There were always some stragglers who had got lost trying to find the right field on the right farm but there was usually enough left for them if and when they found their bearings and arrived.

With autumn it was time for the show itself, always held on the first Saturday in September in a field up the Batsford road, and although only going for seven years, it was already the biggest agricultural show in the county and destined to become one of the biggest of its kind in the country with as fine an entry of hunters, heavy horses, cattle, pigs and sheep as one could see anywhere, and where a cornucopia of flowers, vegetables, cakes, jams and wine was housed in a large marquee, redolent of warm, damp turf. After the show came the annual Mop, squeezing its swings, roundabouts, dodgems and other fairground amusements into High Street for three days, while the weather obligingly confirmed the old local saying, "It always rains on Moreton Mop", by turning wet.

A funny thing happened that October when the gallant little Moreton-in-Marsh fire brigade, volunteers all, responded to a fire alarm at the Fire Service College, created at great expense out of the former RAF Station just up the road, near the Four Shires Stone. When they arrived they found there was no fire at all. The instructors had decided to test the readiness of their students, all full-time firemen, by calling them out on an imaginary fire and the call had been inadvertently relayed outside: hence the arrival of the local brigade. The officers who had a fleet of the most up-to-date fire-fighting vehicles at their disposal, graciously thanked the Moreton-in-Marsh firemen for their prompt assistance, adding, no doubt with tongue in cheek, that it was reassuring to know they could depend on the local brigade in an emergency.

With the coming of winter the pond filled with water again and began to look slightly more respectable. The Redesdale Hall interior was decked with flowers and greenery for its major social event of the year, the Farmers' Ball, where the eats were almost as big an attraction as the dancing after all the rationing during and after the war. As the old year ended and 1957 began, the news came through that the Cotswolds were to be designated an Area of Outstanding Natural Beauty, one of the first to be chosen not for its grandeur but for what Man had done to it with his pleasing geometry of stone boundary walls, dome-shaped clumps of beech trees and towns and villages growing out of the earth as if they were part of it. Unfortunately, the designation threatened Moreton-in-Marsh with another fateful dichotomy because the railway line, which went through the centre of the town, was chosen as the boundary with the result that half the built-up area was protected and the other half, not.

Almost a year had gone by since the parish council decided not to resign or buy the other half of the pond. The media had found other sensations to excite them and the world at large soon forgot all the controversy. Even the parishioners seemed content to ignore the pond and wrap themselves in their usual comfortable shawl of apathy. But a last sensation had still to come! On February 22, 1957, the Cotswold Journal published the glad news: "Moreton Duck Pond No Longer Divided. Parish Council Owns The Lot".

At the previous Tuesday's council meeting a letter had come from Major Summers saying, "Since it is the wish of the parish that the duck pond should remain as a pond and since it seems ridiculous that this water should be divided between two owners, I am willing to offer as an unconditional gift to the council my half of the pond. I sincerely hope that the council will accept this gift and that they and the parish will feel that some good has come out of this affair."

Mr Horne, who must have been as appalled at having a whole pond dumped on the council as he had been at having half of one, managed a smile and magnanimously remarked, "If the pond is to remain as a pond, I suppose it is better that it should be entirely under public ownership."

At the annual parish meeting on March 27, now as sparsely attended as it always used to be, Nelson Newbury, the local milkman, asked what was going to happen to the duck pond now that it belonged entirely to the council.

Mr Horne, who must have been hoping and praying that someone would asked this question, smugly replied, "Surely it is I who ought to be asking that question of you?" He meant that as it was people like Mr Newbury who had wanted to save the pond, it was up to them and not the council to put it right.

Edgar Rolph, as ebullient off the council as he had been on it, said, "Since the parish council seems to be absolutely devoid of ideas for improving their property I would like to propose that they allow a committee outside the council to be formed for the purpose of collecting money and cleaning out the pond," and this was carried.

Such a committee was formed at a special public meeting in the Congregational Hall on Monday, April 24, 1957, with Nelson Newbury as chairman and Edgar Rolph, secretary, and five others, including myself, who immediately set about organising a whist drive for the following Friday to raise funds for cleaning out the pond. After just over two years of argument and action the great Moreton-in-Marsh duck pond saga that had riven a town and stirred the Nation was over.

Perhaps the best summation of the affair came from William Connor, alias Cassandra, the celebrated columnist of the "Daily Mirror", which at that time had the largest circulation of any daily newspaper in the world. He wrote about it on March 21, 1956, when Georgi Malenkov, who had recently succeeded Stalin as dictator of the Soviet Union, was visiting this country and meeting Hugh Gaitskell, leader of the Labour Party, which then formed the official Opposition.

"I don't know what example Mr Gaitskell gave to Mr Malenkov about the workings of the two-party democracy but I hope he didn't overlook the Duck Pond Affair at Moreton-in-Marsh," Cassandra wrote. "In its way it has been a little classic of the opposition saying to authority: 'Oi' You can't do that there 'ere. Which is one of the basic rules of our way of Government.

"It happened like this. The parish council at Moreton-in-Marsh owned half a duck pond - and, as you know, half a duck pond is better than no duck pond at all. In fact, they have owned this 50 per cent of the pond for 130 years. The other half was recently bought by a Major Summers who wishes to fill it up and build lock-up garages on the site. The councillors, all obliging, wanted to sell their half to the Major. But they seem to be rather dull fellows who had never heard of William Allingham on duck ponds,

> *Four ducks on a pond,*
> *A grass bank beyond,*
> *A blue sky of Spring,*
> *White clouds on the wing:*
> *What a little thing*
> *To remember for years –*
> *To remember with tears!*

"Against the tide of local opinion, parish councillors still persisted in trying to get rid of the demi-pond but the parishioners who are - bless 'em! - very duck-minded, promptly rejected the transaction by 132 votes to 59. At the height of the argument at the parish meeting, a duckophile released two ducks from the back of the hall who supplied valuable and cogent quacking. Yet still the council, outvoted and defeated, hung on against the Yeomen of the Cotswolds, but in the words of one of their opponents, Lieutenant commander Clarke-Irons, their days may be numbered. 'We should applaud the decision of the parish council because they are so sure in their minds of their own integrity and we should thank them for their services to the community because it is very likely that after the next election they will not be there to represent us.'

"This is a fight about a duck pond and nearly as small a thing, perhaps, as you could take among our affairs. But it is fought out in the open with all the ingredients of a good British row: anger, humour, bad temper, delight, reason and abuse. Yet let Mr Malenkov with all his savage camps around the Arctic Circle mark this point. Nobody has been thrown into that demi-duck pond and all the violence that has occurred amounts to nothing more than a few ruffled feathers on the backs of half-a-dozen parish councillors at Moreton-in-Marsh."

As for the pond, it resisted all efforts to improve it. The money was easily raised to have it dredged and tidied up but nothing could make it gladden the eye or diminish its majestic scruffiness. As for the council, a year is a long time in parish pump politics and when the next elections came along, all of the old guard who sought re-election were successful though the female element was restored with the election of Miss Drucker, a valued member of our Duck Pond Committee, who held office for many years thereafter.

As for myself, I remained with the Journal for another 25 years or more and the duck pond proved a valuable friend to me. Every district reporter needs an all-weather stand-by to fall back on when news is short and the duck pond, having achieved fame, safely saw me through many a silly season. Anything I wrote about it found an audience among Journal readers because they knew about the pond having become a national cause célèbre and though the world outside had soon forgotten about it, the local population had not.

The pond flooded, it dried up, it froze and people skated on it, boys boated on it and fell in it, ducks were put on it and vanished from it, specially near Christmas-time when they ended up in someone's pot, ducks perished crossing the road to or from it, oil seeped into it, ducks got oil on their wings from it, the RSPCA investigated it, a Warwickshire man said something strange lay under it, swans settled on it and fought on it, including a male which drove its adversary under the wheels of a passing car, vandals tossed kerbing stones in it, citizens chafed as the sheer unsightliness of it, public money was spent on improving it, ratepayers complained at the cost of it… There was no end to the stories the pond provided.

I see you've sent through another duck pond story," the Editor would telephone to say. "Short of news, are we?" But he always used it! So let this account be regarded as a vote of thanks to that dear old ugly duck pond, which may sometimes have run out of water but never out of newsworthiness, from one who was its beneficiary.

Our guinea pig died in that plane crash

WEIGHING IT UP

...essing the weight of a
used to be bad enough.
always guess was so far
that only politeness
vented the competition
ganiser from having hys-
rics. But these weight-
essing contests are getting
ven more challenging. At
Blockley Flower Show it was
a question of guessing the
weight of a pair of fantail
doves, and at the Moreton
Show, guessing the weight of
a Friesian cow called Albert.

One would have thought
the margin of error with a
cow would have been enor-
mous, but the fact is that
Mr. Williams, of Peach
Cottages, Idicote,

r guinea pig was killed in that
Aer Lingus plane crash over
h Sea the week before last.
rd the aircraft, said the
pers, was Mr. William
a director of the Gilbert
n Opera For All Com-
for 17 years musical
e D'Oyly Carte
near th a distri-
exact

a reference to the churned-up condition of the estate due to so many
strangers descending on it. The
motto adorned a heraldic shield
supported by two h   (for Hogsnorton) in   ts and dis-
plavin   a bunch of
                 us and a
                hly means
                to the
              too,
            nterest
           We
        ed:
       Life,
       I
     happ
    tryis
   ifes
   use
  sur
  red
  fin

and her make-up was pretty advanced for those days. To watch
her applying it with the same
artistry she gave to one of her
drawings was a fascination, though
I risked   nose daubed
with   inquisi-

They
called
an op
eyes,
very
worth
of it
one

Down at the front

as like turning back
k last Saturday when
stances obliged me to
the matinee perform-
of "The Fall of the
Empire" at the Re
when normally I would
gone to an evening per-
nance.

now have to sit much
ser to the screen than I used
do—a sign of advancing
ars?—and thus found myself
tting close to that band of
mps which has traditionally
occupied the front rows of the
stalls at Saturday matinees
and of which I was once proud
to boast myself a member.

Other ex-members who have
now graduated to the back
rows, the balcony or—traitors!
—to television will be glad to
know that things have not
        much down at the

occupiers are much as we
were.

There is still the know-all
who wishes to demonstrate his
prescience to his fellow eight-
year-olds by forecasting the
plot, and who is very rarely
right. "These are the Romans,"
he said confidently. "They'll
win." (They lost.) "This is
where his chariot wheel comes
off." (It didn't.) "You watch,
he'll hit him." (He missed.)
Undaunted, he continued
with his malpredictions.

At first I was puzzled by
stealthy sounds and move-
ments approaching me during
the performance but I should
not have been. I quickly
realised that this was an undercover safari crawling upwards from the front rows to
the better seats at the back.
They decided they had come
far enough when they reached
me and settled down in my
vicinity. I think they were
    ing to use me as camou-

on the scene telling them to
return from whence they came.
Here, the situation was different from yesteryear. We
used to go back as meekly as
lambs but not this lot! The
usherette fought a hard battle
with much imperious torch-
flashing but, like the Roman
Empire, she was doomed to
fall and eventually retired to
base.

Neither Marcus Aurelius
nor his legions could have
shifted this little knot of Barbarians.

The only other change lay in
myself. When people in the
film got a lance through their
chest or a sword in their gizzard I winced, as is my wor
and looked away. Not so
juveniles. It would be ha
exaggerate the intense pl
that such spectacles gav
It was almost as if
had reached from t
and given them
Christmas present.
Obviously   we
much to learn ab
                to viol

TROUBLE FOR THE 5.15 FROM PADDINGTON

MORETON - IN - MARSH's most
fashionable train—the 5.15 p.m.
out of Paddington on Fridays,
bringing the elite of the district
to the Cotswolds for the week-
end—ran into trouble last Friday
when it came to a halt about 200
yards short of the station.
Knights,   city
financiers, past and present, debutantes,   company
with the problem of being so near
and yet so far, decided to complete the rest of the journey on
foot. Numbering 63 in all, they
threaded their way along the track
towards the platform, where their
waiting cars, turn Moreton's station yard into a miniature motor show
on Friday evenings, gazed helplessly on.

The cause of the trouble was a diesel
train which caught fire while
stationary at the down platform.
The fire was put out by the driver
and station staff but it put the
diesel out of action. When the
5.15 p.m Paddington t
shortly before

CHOIRMASTER TO 100,000

  rable of
he talents

The Rev. John Davey, who is rec-
of the Rissingtons, has been giv-
£1 notes away on the understand-
they are used to make money for
 church. For example, his
arishioners can buy ingredients for
akes to make and sell, or use the
money to invest in some other profit-
making enterprise.

The idea is not new. The Scouts and
Guides have been doing it for years,
not just to raise money but as a test
of initiative. It is less common among

the
tch
ng
re
n

What is it like to be choirmaster
to 100,000 people?

"I am a little apprehensive before
I go on," says Mr. Rea. "I just hope
that the crowd will be with me. You
must realise that you cannot completely control a crowd of 100,000.
They are not going to keep exactly
in tune and they may drag a bit.
Somehow, you have to keep them
together. Some crowds are more
amenable to discipline than others.
If this year's is as good as last
year's, I shall be very happy."

A native of Northern Ireland, Mr.
Rea has lived at Chipping Norton
for seven years. He is hoping to sell
 he cafe shortly and retire. He plays
 violin, saxophone and clarinet, and
 s been a band leader on P. & O.
  mers, musical director of the Belfast

right sort of
compering
orchestras
though I h
This Wem
really."

Has an
Wembley
the sing
High.

someon
pitch a
he w

Mr.
tells
goin
him
com
bac

INNOCENT EAVESDROPPER Gets 'Phone Calls on Radio

Mrs. Elizabeth Young, farmer's wife,
of Clapton-on-the-Hill, near Bourton-on-
the-Water, keeps hearing her neighbour's telephone conversations when she
switches on the B.B.C. Light Programme.
If it is a quiet programme she can hear
almost every word they say. She has
complained to the Post Office about
investigating the curious behaviour of
her radio set.

It was several weeks ago that Mrs.
Young first heard the tone of a telephone call signal on her radio. Then,
during a lull between programmes, she
heard the lifting of a telephone receiver
and recognised the voice of a young
     neighbour.
When she told him about it he laughed.
When her radio continued to pick
up other telephone conversations, Mrs.
Young felt things were getting beyond a
joke. She reported the matter to the
Post Office who told her that the case
was an unusual one and might take some
time to put right.

Et Cetera

A Miscellany from the Cotswold Journal 1954-8

INTER–CHORAL FEUDING

The monks of Evesham Abbey had no idea what trouble they were laying in store for future generations when they allowed two churches to go up in the same churchyard. For two churches meant two sets of choirboys and to use the Western clichè no churchyard was big enough to hold the both of them.

In my time the inter-choral feud was vigorously pursued as it was no doubt before and has been since. Being of the All Saints' faction I may of course be partial but the St Lawrence' lot always seemed bigger and more bellicose than we were.

They of course were Low Church. We were High. It was an unusual arrangement - was it not? - to have the two churches providing for the opposite extremes of devotional inclination yet served by the same clergy.

The St Lawrence' boys were not much interested in dogma or liturgical niceties but they knew incense when they could smell it and did not approve. Not only were our cassocks redolent of it but our walking-out clothes too and the result was a constant olfactory provocation.

As I was one of two eight-year-old acolytes, who wore red cassocks, it was to a certain extent advisable to encourage the animosity towards St Lawrence's because the All Saints' choirboys in purple cassocks were not beyond turning on us like birds do against their own kind dressed in wrong plumage.

Oh, what adventures we used to have in the darkening churchyard under the light of a frosty moon! The two choirs never met host against host as it were. The idea was to waylay unwary stragglers from the other side. One evening we had an ambush set up in the pitch dark and as our victim's footsteps reached us we leapt on him holding our macs like the nets of the retiarii only to find that we had captured the curate! His first words on recovering himself - and I remember them well - were: "This is an irreverent scandal!" spoken with immense indignation.

When the war came and the black-out was nightly imposed on us this added to the excitement. I would not walk the churchyard alone after dark not for fear of ghoulies and ghosties but lest others of the rival faction were hiding behind a tombstone to get me.

The black-out had other perils. They managed to black out the chancel of All Saints' but were defeated by the nave and transepts. One evening at a rehearsal for a particularly high High Feast Day involving a new and complex processional route, crucifer, choir and clergy set off into the inkiness of the nave, hoping that they would manage to find their way, but they certainly did not. Amid much crashing into pews and collision with each other could be heard the Vicar's voice calling for torches and rescue.

The flashpoint of the year was the annual choir outing by train to Weymouth. All went well on the outward journey and during the day on beach and promenade but on the return journey when we fell to carousing on American cream soda or dandelion and burdock, woe betide the solitary wanderer who might find himself captured and given a taste of the Chinese burn!

Another wheeze was vigorously to shake a pop bottle, open the door of an enemy compartment and let its contents soar in an effervescent fountain upon them. Let it be added that we did no damage to the train, only to ourselves nor did animosity survive into later life or even after our voices broke.

Once a year found the two choirs united, not against a common foe but a common danger. This was on Ascension Day when we used to climb the 110ft Bell Tower to sing a hymn from the top. A church service started at 6.45 am and was supposed to be over between half-past seven and a quarter-to-eight but it usually overran with the result that the choirboys, never so much at one as when in mutual terror, were climbing through the vast bell chamber when the clock struck eight.

It was bad enough having to go up those winding stone steps in cassocks but to be on the ladder in the belfry with the clock striking was horrendous. Not, only was the noise of the bells deafening but the very wooden rungs used to shake. It was like being up a mainmast in a thunderstorm at sea.

After that, though, it was lovely. To stand on top of the tower singing "Hail the day that sees Him rise" with the birds wheeling below in the clean morning sunlight and the quiet town still shrugging off its late slumber was an unforgettable experience. What a pity the old custom no longer survives!

1979

ON THE MOVE WITH GEORGE

No ordinary mortal can have received such a spectacular tribute as the late George Henry Hewins is now being given in his native town of Stratford-upon-Avon. Nor has he had to wait a generation or more after his death to be so honoured. He died only six years ago at the age of 98 and many remember him if only by sight.

Why George Hewins, a barely literate man whose life was spent for the most part in utter poverty? The reason is that like so many of his humble station he could recall the past with fluency and wit and his grandson's wife had the good sense to tape record what he said and publish it in written form in a book of his early life called "The Dillen". The word means the smallest of the litter and was a name given to George who was only 5ft 3ins tall.

That book has now been adapted for the stage by Ron Hutchinson and is being presented by the Royal Shakespeare Theatre in a manner unparalleled in the history of the British Theatre. The Chorus in "Henry V" by George's fellow townsman bemoans that his play must be presented in a wooden cockpit when a kingdom is needed for a stage. Barry Kyle, the director of "The Dillen" is not so inhibited

He opens the play in the company's studio theatre, then goes out-of-doors to use the highways and byways of the town as a platform for George's story. It is a sensational moment when the doors of the theatre are flung open letting in the daylight and what appears to be half the population of Stratford dressed in Victorian costume and singing George Hewins' song. When they go we can do naught but follow.

In the gardens opposite the theatre "Black George", the Stratford vicar of George's youth, presides over the church school, where the girls are being given sewing chores to do while the boys provide a counterpoint performing their drill outside.

At the junction of Trinity Street and College Lane we come across two bobbies wrestling with the young George who has been up to mischief and who is only rescued in the nick of time by his beloved great Aunt Cal, herself travelling on a red horse-drawn omnibus. Wherever the actors go the audience goes too.

Film makers regularly use a real town or city to give credence or atmosphere to a story but never before has a live theatrical performance taken to the streets this way and made use of a place as Stratford is being used: not, one must add, the popular centre of the town but for the most part the less fashionable areas as befits a tale of poverty and hard work.

And to enhance this local dimension Mr Kyle has recruited 200 local people as extras - George was himself an extra or "super", as he called it, at the theatre at one time - and it is a tribute to both elements of the cast that it is hard to tell where the professionals end and the amateurs begin so convincingly are they mixed together.

There is only one well-known player and this is Peggy Mount who is truly worth her not inconsiderable weight in gold. As Cal Cook, who lived on the corner of Sheep Street and Waterside and lovingly raised George after his mother deserted him, she not only gives an appropriately warm-hearted performance but by the power of her presence holds the entire peripatetic production together, a Rock of Gibraltar figure whom the audience turns to just as George did as a lad.

He is presented in boyhood, as a young man and in old age, the latter condition being touchingly depicted by Dickie Arnold who looks George to the life. But it is Ron Cook who has the bulk of the work to do as George, the young man, and he creates a vivid character, unafraid to look poverty in the face and spit it in the eye.

Does it all work? If Mr Kyle, who is known to have a keen social conscience, believes that greater realism can be achieved by moving out-of-doors he is mistaken. It is all too jolly and too picturesque. A film can convey the detail of squalor and deprivation more effectively: so can a clever stage designer with an interior set. Nor to be truthful does the production convince us that this is George as he really was, warts and all. The myth is already beginning to take over from the man.

Where the production succeeds overwhelmingly is in its presentation. We participated in a visual adventure rather like going on an on-foot sightseeing tour. As we swing the last corner of Mill Lane and see the railway bridge across the Avon, there are a couple in all their Victorian finery lolling in a rowing boat on the river, a lovely sight. As we mount the bridge and look to the Clifford Chambers bank there is a field of women pea-pickers looking for all the world like peasants in a Millet painting. When they are cheated by their foreman they throw him into the river, literally! He goes in with a splash!

The producer successfully links these various scenes, which are often some distance apart, by having a brass band to lead us from one place to another and by allowing the actors to throw away dialogue while already on the move.

Not until after the interval does our attention wander. The Great War scenes seem extraneous and over-familiar though it is dark now and with the guns pounding and shells exploding it is not difficult to imagine the Hun crawling towards us through the long grass from Welford Way. The war scenes are justified, perhaps, when on the return journey we stop at Stratford War Memorial, a pillar among a sea of flaming torches, to hear the names of the Fallen spoken: it is good to hear their names remembered. By the closing scene we are back in the theatre again with the badly wounded George being offered yet another soul-destroying job in the good name of charity. The country fit for heroes to live in is the same onerous place for him that it has always been.

1983

CHOIRMASTER TO 100,000

Almost as much a part of the Wembley Cup Final as the match itself is the community singing that precedes it. Shortly before the match is due to start a man in a white suit climbs a 12ft high rostrum and while a Service band plays conducts what must be the biggest choir in the world - 100,000 people.

By tradition the programme ends with the hymn, "Abide With Me", always a moving experience. When West Bromwich Albion meet Everton in the final this Saturday the songs will include "Congratulations", Britain's choice for the Eurovision Song Contest, and "Thank You Very Much" requested by Everton supporters. The musicians will be the Band of the Royal Marines, Portsmouth, and the man in the white suit will be as usual, Frank Rea, of The Phoenix Cafe, Chipping Norton.

"What is it like to be choirmaster to 100,000 people?"

"I am a little apprehensive before I go on," says Mr Rea. "I just hope that the crowd will be with me. You must realise that you cannot completely control a crowd of 100,000. They are not going to keep exactly in tune and they may drag a bit. Somehow you have to keep them together. Some crowds are more amenable to discipline than others. If this year's is as good as last year's I shall be very happy."

Born in Northern Ireland Mr Rea has lived at Chipping Norton for seven years. He plays the violin, saxophone and clarinet and has been a band leader on P & O liners, musical director of the Belfast Opera House and a broadcaster. How did he come to get the Wembley job?

"I was asked whether I would do it," he says. "I suppose I had the right sort of experience. I have been compèring shows and conducting orchestras for most of my life though I have retired from it now. This Wembley job is all I do now, really."

Has anything ever gone wrong at Wembley?

"On one occasion during the singing of "Looking High, High, Looking Low, Low, Low" someone managed to get across the pitch and before I knew where I was he was up on the rostrum beside me. This is when your experience tells. I managed to keep the singing going and at the same time persuade him to go away. He eventually went back of his own free will. How he managed to get there I don't know!"

Mr Rea admits that he is not particularly football minded and prefers cricket. After the community singing he never stops to watch the final. "I have to get back to Chipping, Norton to my business," he says.

1968

TEMPERAMENTAL MIKES

Why do they have to have new-fangled things like microphones at such time-honoured homely events as village fetes? Can't people shout any more? Apart from the fact that these sinuous, cobra-like contraptions look totally out of place in a traditional setting of lawns and mellow garden walls, the things never seem to work! The charming lady who is to declare the fete open steps forward to make her little speech into the microphone and what happens? Her lips move but nothing is heard from the loudspeakers. A check is made of the wires and cables, plugs are pulled and switches thrown, until the signal is given for her to step forward again. But do we hear her voice? No! This time the air is rent with such metallic shrieks and squealing that one might be forgiven for thinking that Martians had landed in the herbaceous border. At the third attempt we hear her voice at last, at first very far away, then very near, then very soft, then deafening, then basso profundo, then piping treble, while o'er the air a syrupy humming hangs. One's mental picture of a typical English fete used to be of flags against the trees, decorated stalls on green lawns and teas on the terrace. How it is more likely to be of some desperate individual, usually a clergyman, shouting into a microphone: 'Can you hear me? Can you hear me?" And, of course, nobody can!

1966

PARABLE OF THE TALENTS

The Rev John Davey, who is rector of the Rissingtons, has been giving £1 notes away on the understanding they are used to make money for the church. For example his parishioners can buy ingredients for cakes to make and sell, or use the money to invest in some other profit-making enterprise.

The idea is not new. The Scouts and Guides have been doing it for years, not just to raise money but as a test of initiative. It is less common among adults. Giving a man £1 to speculate with could be asking for trouble. It might easily end up in a bookmaker's pocket after being squandered on an also-ran at the races.

The idea springs of course from the parable of the three servants, which I have always found one of the most chilling parts of the New Testament. I get a horrible feeling in the pit of my stomach each time I hear it, being convinced every word is aimed at me.

If you remember, a master who is going away gives bags of money to three servants to look after in his absence. The first servant gets five bags, the second two and the third servant one. The first servant succeeds in doubling the number of his bags; so does the second servant. The third servant, who has carefully hidden the money, has only the one bag to offer when the master returns.

I must say I find the master's reaction quite inexplicable. Instead of rebuking the first two servants for gambling with his money and risking losing it all, he praises and promotes them. The third servant he not only chastises but - and I quote - takes from him the little he has and casts him into outer darkness, a place of weeping and gnashing of teeth.

As you have probably deduced I find myself completely identifying with the cautious servant who comes to such a bad end. If a friend were to give me £50 to look after I would certainly not use it for barter or to invest on the stock market. Nor would I put it in a building society because even those have been known to go bust before now.

No, I would put it in some safe place till he was ready and asked for it back though apparently this would be a very wrong thing to do. I got so worried about this that at one time I wrote to the question-and-answer column in a religious magazine asking for enlightenment. The reply I got was so obscure that I couldn't understand a word of it. Nor, I suspect, did the expert who wrote it.

This parable seems a perfect justification for capitalism red in tooth and claw. No wonder the prosperous Victorians could go to church in droves with a clear conscience when they heard it delivered to them from the lectern! Why worry about their underpaid, overworked servants when all those gold pieces were being merrily multiplied for the master?

There was a straw that I used to clutch at. In the Authorised Version the gold pieces were referred to as talents, an old name for money, and I decided to take the word at its contemporary face value namely as a natural gift capable of being developed. Very few people have real talent but all of us presumably have the ability to be kind to one another, and so I took what modicum of kindness I had and tried to multiply it into a thriving concern and respect for my fellow man. A talent for caring, you might say. Alas! That escape is now denied me. The modern English version of the New Testament refers unequivocally to bags of gold. There is no mention of talents at all.

I gather Mr Davey's scheme is going very well and that he has already netted over £200 from his initial distribution of free £1 notes. What interests me though is what he is going to do with those people who have only got their original £1 or worse still who have lost the lot as a result of their transactions? Does Outer Darkness beckon?

1981

DOWN AT THE FRONT

It was like turning back the clock last Saturday when circumstances obliged me to attend the matinee performance of "The Fall Of The Roman Empire" at the Regal cinema when normally I would have gone to an evening performance.

I now have to sit much nearer the screen than I used to - a sign of advancing years? - and thus found myself sitting close to that band of imps which has traditionally occupied the front rows of the stalls at Saturday matinees and of which I was once proud to boast myself a member.

Other ex-members who have now graduated to the back rows, the balcony or - traitors! - to television will be glad to know that things have not changed much down at the front. There is a good deal more guzzling of orangeade and licking of lollies going on: in our day we got threepence for our seat and that was our lot. But otherwise the present occupiers are much as we were.

There is still the know-all who wishes to demonstrate his prescience to his fellow eight-year-olds by forecasting the plot and who proves very rarely right. "These are the Romans," he said confidently. "They'll win." (They lost). "This is where his chariot wheel comes off." (It didn't). "You watch, he'll hit him." (He missed). Undaunted he continued with his malpredictions.

At first I was puzzled by stealthy sounds and movements approaching me during the performance but I should not have been. I quickly realised that this was an undercover safari crawling upwards from the front seats to the better seats at the back. They decided they had come far enough when they reached me and settled down in my vicinity. I think they were hoping to use me as camouflage.

If so they were disappointed because an usherette was soon on the scene telling them to return from whence they came. Here, the situation was different from yesteryear. We used to go back meekly as lambs but not this lot! The usherette fought a hard battle with much imperious torch flashing but like the Roman Empire she was doomed to fall and eventually retired to base defeated. Neither Marcus Aurelius nor his legions could have shifted this little knot of Barbarians!

The only other change lay in myself. When people in the film got a lance through their chest or a sword in their gizzard I winced as is my wont and looked away. Not so the juveniles. It would be hard to exaggerate the delight that such spectacles gave them. It was almost as if someone had reached from the screen and given them a belated Christmas present. Obviously we still have much to learn about children's reaction to violence.

1969

SUMMER RESORT FOR TRAMPS

It is almost as if the gods decided that as Chipping Campden was so beautiful it should pay the price by having an annual scourge visited upon it. The symptoms appear in the late spring when the first crops are beginning to ripen and do not subside until the mist of autumn has put a frosty nip in the air.

Suddenly one spring afternoon you are walking along a footpath or quiet lane and you spot it: not the first cuckoo or the first primrose but a bundle of old clothes which proves to be a human being sleeping off the effects of his midday beverage. The first roadster of the season has arrived.

The majority of casual workers, pea pickers - call them what you will - are no doubt sober and conscientious people otherwise the local farmers would not employ them but the influx at Campden during the harvesting season includes some who must be regarded as the fag ends of humanity.

Their support - and their downfall - is alcohol and they eke out their existence living homeless and rootless by earning enough money to drown their sorrows in cider and then find some secluded place whereon to sink into a soporific oblivion for the rest of the afternoon or evening.

To have to walk past one or more of these men when they are in this inebriated state is unpleasant for a man: for a woman it must be intolerable. They shout at you but it is hard to understand what they say: they could be trying to be friendly or they could be abusive. A number of complaints have been made by residents who have been so accosted.

Campden seems to be unique among North Cotswold communities in being a summer resort for the roadster type of person. Where he gets to during the winter is anyone's guess. He and his fellows have been spending their summers there for so long that they are now largely taken for granted despite the occasional complaint to the parish council or police.

Yet if it were happening for the first time this very year many might think it a public scandal. A few years ago one of the roadsters was burnt to death in a barn where he was sleeping and where it seems likely he was the inadvertent cause of the fire that engulfed him. Another's decomposing body was found in a lonely place, the only clue as to when he died being the date on the newspaper on which his body was lying. Another was run over and killed while lying inert in the middle of the road at night.

The police obviously have a recurring problem on their hands. To a certain extent they try to be tolerant but they are firm when necessary: several men have already been sent to prison for drunkenness so far this summer and another who assaulted the landlady of a local pub by hitting her across the face with a bottle was also gaoled. Another was sent to a mental hospital after committing an unnatural offence with an animal. There seems little more that either the police or the local council can do.

The answer really lies with society as a whole to find out why these men cannot put down roots, exist without alcohol or do more than fritter their lives away. A few may be the gentlemen of the road of the days of yore: the tramps who reject society in order to live a life of freedom under the open sky going where they will. But the majority seem to have the unhappy look of misfits on the run.

Leniency when they come before the magistrates is fruitless because they have no home address or money in their possession to pay even the smallest fine. To take any other course but sending them to prison is impracticable when they come and go like shadows and are impossible to supervise.

A visitor to Campden once wrote to the parish council complaining that the town was a vile place for snobbery after she had seen a notice in a public house saying: No pea pickers served here. "If she and other socially minded people were to devote their efforts to discovering how to keep such people as the publican had in mind, out of the pubs instead of wishing to make it easier for them to enter, she and they would be doing both society and Campden a good turn.

1967

DEATH OF A GUINEA PIG

Our guinea pig died in that Aer Lingus plane crash over the Irish Sea last week. On board the aircraft, said the daily papers, was William Cox-Ife, a director of the Gilbert and Sullivan Opera For All Company and for 17 years musical director of the D'Oyly Carte Opera Company. With a distinctive name like that there could be no doubt about it. It was our guinea pig all right.

He and his wife flashed across my life like a pair of meteors when I was a small boy and I can' t think of anyone who has had so much influence on me in so short a time. Mr Cox-Ife was one of the BBC Men's Chorus which was evacuated to Wood Norton, near Evesham, at the outbreak of the Second World War and he and his wife were billeted on us.

They were called guinea pigs because this was the nickname given to all the BBC billetees, who were supplied with bed and breakfast for seven days a week at a universal rate of one guinea per week.

Mr Cox-Ife's eyes lit up when he saw our front room. "Ah, a piano!" he exclaimed and for the few months he was with us we were treated to professional piano playing and singing such as we had never heard before. Often his BBC friends would join him in the front room for concerts that still echo across the years. Some were famous people who would have cost a huge sum to hire professionally.

That first Christmas of the war it was he who conceived the Latin motto on the Wood Norton Christmas card: *Nec Glaur Terrent*, meaning they were not deterred by mud, a reference to the churned up condition of the estate due to so many strangers descending on it. The motto adorned a heraldic shield supported by two hogs (for Hogsnorton, a fictional destination heard about on pre-war radio) and displaying such devices as a bunch of Vale of Evesham asparagus and a triptych of bicycles, the only means of getting to and from Evesham at that time.

Mrs Cox-Ife was a fashion artist for "Woman's Weekly". After seeing clothes which the magazine wished to promote, she would do line and wash figure drawings showing what the clothes would look like when they were worn. It was a skilled art which she did extremely well. She showed me the professional way of drawing a woman in semi-profile and I still find myself doing this when doodling.

By old Evesham standards they were a very Bohemian couple: easygoing, impulsive and extravagant. On the quiet they used to give me more pocket money than my parents did. They were also striking to look at. Mr Cox-Ife, who was over 6ft tall, was only just turned 30 but his thick hair was already silver. His wife dressed colourfully and her make-up was pretty advanced for those days. To watch her applying it with the same artistry she gave to her drawings was a fascination.

They had a white Persian cat called Lakmè after a character in an opera. It had beautiful blue eyes, which apparently made it quite rare, and was said to be worth £100. We went in fear of inadvertently letting it out and one afternoon when the inevitable happened, spent a worried hour trying to coax all £100 of it from the roof. When we knew the Cox-Ifes were out for the evening we used to borrow Lakmè for the pleasure of her company but she was really too haughty a creature to find us socially acceptable.

Eventually the couple moved to their own flat in High Street and we were allocated other guinea pigs though none anywhere near as exciting as our first had been. They then left the district when Mr Cox-Ife volunteered or was called up for the Army and I never saw either of them again. Mrs Cox-Ife died several years later and her husband remarried.

Although I had the chance of looking him up several times when he was with the D'Oyly Carte Company at Stratford, I chose not to do so because I did not want to see him through adult eyes. I know he would have been glad to see me but I wanted to remember him as he had seemed to me as a child: glamorous, richly talented, larger than life and quite unlike anyone I had ever known before. His death in the grey Irish Sea will not wash this image away.

1968

GUESSING THE WEIGHT

Guessing the weight of a cake used to be bad enough. One always had the feeling that one's guess was so far out that only politeness prevented the competition organiser from bursting out laughing. But these weight guessing contests are getting even more challenging. At Blockley flower show it was a question of guessing the weight of a pair of fantail doves and at the Moreton Show, the weight of a Friesian cow called Albert.

One would have thought that the margin for error with a cow would have been enormous but the fact is that a Mr Williams, of Peach Cottages, Idlicote, near Shipston-on-Stour, guessed its exact weight: 918½lbs. Moreover, Mrs Pulley, of Sezincote, near Moreton, who guessed 918lbs was only half-a-pound out and several others guessed 920lbs. Those who dread making fools of themselves can take comfort that the lowest weight guessed was 360lbs, less than half the correct weight, and the highest, 1,700lbs, nearly double.

1970

MASTER HORNBLOWER

In the North Cotswolds the undisputed virtuoso of the hunting horn and coaching horn, the musical long and short of it as you might say, is Martin Dee, who farms at Park Farm, Blockley.

He is the present holder of both the hunting horn and coaching horn championships at the Chequers Inn, Churchill, where a horn blowing contest is held each December, and he is the winner of the Heythrop Hunt Supporters' Club annual hunting horn contest too.

Whence comes Mr Dee's prowess at these two instruments from which the average person could not get a note no matter how hard he tried? Is it all a question of wind power? "No, it's practice," says Mr Dee, whose home is fortunately far from other habitation. "I practice during the winter for five minutes every night."

He started blowing the bugle in Blockley's St John Ambulance band as a lad during the Second World War. "Then I went to this dance and someone had a hunting horn and let me have a go on it," he explains, "and it was dead simple after a bugle."

Round about this time he joined Moreton-in-Marsh Young Farmers' Club and at the YFC county balls at Cheltenham or Gloucester the band leader used to hold a competition to see which young farmer could blow the longest on the hunting horn, a feat at which Mr Dee excelled. "He always said I blew 55 seconds at one go," he says, "but I have my doubts about that. I have never blown more than 50 seconds since then."

Mr Dee's first serious experience of competitive blowing was at a Hereford hunt ball in the early 1950s when he got two second prizes. "Someone suggested I was quite good and that I ought to get some coaching," he says. "I saw Captain Wallace MFH and he agreed to coach me and taught me all I know. I owe all my success to him."

Since then Mr Dee has gone from one pulmonary success to another. At a "Horse and Hound" ball in London he blew shoulder to shoulder with Jimmy Edwards, the comedian, no mean horn blower himself. At a Lechlade horn blowing competition he won the amateur section and was then urged to try his luck in the professional section against huntsmen and masters. He won that too.

He has won the Bicester and Warden Hill hunt competition three years in a row and did the same with the West Warwickshire. Such competitions require a challenger to blow a call of his own choice, then one asked for by the judges. There are many different hunting calls such as "Moving Off", "Found a fox" and "Crossing the ride." The judges sit in an adjoining room to hear the calls so as not to know the identity of the challenger.

Mr Dee agrees that the hunting horn, nine inches long, is easier to play than the coaching horn, all of five feet long. However he can muster a tune on the latter instrument, including the "Posthorn Gallop" and "A-hunting We Will Go."

"It is no use just blowing like mad," says Mr Dee, who is a regular cigarette smoker. "It is an art that comes with practice." The game is not without its hazards. It is not uncommon for one's lip to give way or even split. One of the benefits of regular practice is that it hardens the lips.

After all his success is Mr Dee thinking of hanging up his coaching horn and his hunting horn and giving his lungs a rest? "Not likely!" he says. "I'm just getting into my prime."

1976

ELUSIVE CHURCH

The little church of Cornwell, a small village near Chipping Norton, looks very inviting on its hillock among the trees but for the unwary stranger it is an invitation to be accepted with caution.

Having glimpsed the church from the lane many times over the years I decided the time had come last week-end for me, an inveterate church bagger with his name in innumerable visitors' books, to interrupt my journey from Chipping Norton and go in search of the building.

This proved more difficult than expected. One gets used to country churches being across a field, in a farmyard or hidden in the pocket of a great house but Cornwell church was the most elusive I have yet come across. By the time I had circumnavigated the village thrice it was obvious there was absolutely no official way of getting to the church at all.

I had better explain that Cornwell is one of those villages dominated by its manor house, whose tentacles stretch out in all directions. The view of the south front as seen through ornamental iron gates from the lane is one of the prettiest glimpses in North Oxfordshire and well worth stopping for: a quiet pool in the foreground, dignified facade beyond and lashings of foliage all round.

And whichever way I tried approaching the church I was confronted with manorial property inexorably labelled: "Private Property. No Admittance." But I, as ruthless a church bagger as ever strode a chancel floor, was not to be deterred. I knocked on a cottage door and demanded to know how in the name of John Betjeman one found one's way to the church.

She - for the occupier was a woman - told me to go down the drive to the manor, turn left past the dovecote and take the path across the field. At first I followed her instructions diligently, even to the extent of ignoring the "Private" notice at the entrance to the drive, and found the dovecote, a charming structure in the centre of a broad stabling yard, as architecturally satisfying as a small piazza.

From the piazza I stepped into what looked disconcertingly like the backyard of the manor and here I went seriously wrong. I think the woman must have told me to follow a tall yew hedge. Instead I tried taking what was indubitably the direct route to the church only to land up under a drawing room window in an enclosed walled pleasaunce which was obviously very, very private.

I got out through a low door in the wall as quickly as I could and at last found myself on a path that to an experienced eye proclaimed itself immediately as a church way. I followed this path through an avenue of young trees which will make a fine sight one of these days and was gratified to see the church before me on its hillock a field away.

My walk took me past the east front of the manor and I could not help thinking that if the squire in olden days found it an advantage to have the parish church in his garden it must prove an intolerable nuisance now. Hence no doubt all those "Private" notices everywhere.

When I got to the church it was locked of course but as an experienced church bagger I had no difficulty in finding the key. There is something heartwarmingly consistent about the ecclesiastical mind when it comes to finding a hiding place for keys. And - lo! - after all my wanderings I swung open the church door and stepped inside.

Was it worth the effort? Quite honestly no. It is a small plain church with walls as thick as only the Normans could build them and a chancel arch that mixed both Norman and Pointed together. Its most interesting monument was a wall tablet erected by his relict commemorating "Sir Fairmeadow Penyston, Bart, the last of the male line of this ancient family, who died on 24th December, 1705." Fairmeadow! What a name to give anyone! I wonder if his friends called him Fairy?

INNOCENT EAVESDROPPER

Mrs Elizabeth Young, a farmer's wife of Clapton-on-the-Hill, near Bourton-on-the-Water, keeps hearing her neighbours' telephone conversations when she switches on the BBC Light Programme. If it's a quiet radio programme she can hear almost every word they say. She has complained to the Post Office who are investigating the curious behaviour of her radio set.

It was several weeks ago that Mrs Young first heard a telephone call signal on her radio. Then during a lull between programmes she heard the lifting of a telephone receiver and recognised the voice of a neighbour, Ernest Reeves, speaking to a friend.

When she told him about it he laughed but when her radio continued to pick up other telephone conversations Mrs Young felt things were getting beyond a joke. She raised the matter with the Post Office who told her the case was an unusual one and might take some time to put right. It did.

1954

THRILL OF THE AUCTION

Nothing stimulates country people more than a good auction sale. Indeed there is a strong case for claiming it to be the most popular of country pursuits and one that seems to appeal to all classes. Go to a country auction and you will find as perfect a cross-section of village life as you are likely to see under one roof.

What is the fascination of an auction? Obviously the chance of picking up a bargain but there is more to it than that. There is the satisfaction of spotting a treasure among the junk or of uncovering something for which you have been looking for ages, and there is the excitement of the auction itself: of being a spectator at a bidding duel or even a participant with thumping heart and diminishing purse.

Basically the appeal of an auction is very similar to that of another country pastime, the hunt, though fortunately no blood is spilt at the end of it, not often anyway. To see the crowd unleashed on viewing day is like watching the hounds in full cry and when the bidding starts, this is the culmination of the chase, the time to go for the kill.

One of the hazards of going to an auction is that you invariably come away with something you had not dreamt of wanting before you arrived. This may be the reason why some country homes are over-stocked with furniture, many pieces still bearing their tell-tale lot number stubs, so that to negotiate their rooms is like forging through the bush. After all, why pass up a bargain just because you have three or four of the articles in question already in your possession?

There is of course the more publicised auction where the goods are of exceptional value, the prices high and the clientèle more distinguished than usual but with the growth of interest in antiques there is a trend for the two types of sale to merge, so that you may find professional dealers on the look out for objets d'art rubbing shoulders with a cottager in search of a kitchen cabinet.

Moreton-in-Marsh is one of the places where such sales sometimes occur under the aegis of Sheldon Bosley's, and last Thursday's sale was a good example. "Antiques mainly mid-late 18th century, Georgian and Early Victorian, and four lots of Georgian and other silver ware" were balanced by the usual "good quality kitchen utensils and sundries, good quality blankets and curtains." There was something for everyone.

An indication of the importance of the sale was that a 24-hour guard was maintained before the auction with regular checks by the police and on the viewing day at least 800 people were estimated to have visited the showroom. For the auctioneer, Mr Drury, there were just over 500 lots to be disposed of, the result being a six-hour non-stop selling marathon from 11am till five, which left him sore-throated but unbowed.

The sales take place in the auditorium of the former Playhouse Cinema and a bulging Corinthian pilaster here and there hints at the building's romantic past. (How many happy Cotswold unions have originated in the back row of the stalls?) That the building is now used for auctions is a good example of life 's continuity. Where audiences once thrilled to the daring of Buffalo Bill or the Bengal Lancers, they now respond in equal measure to the virtuosity of John Gray Drury FAI and his auctioneer's hammer!

1969

THE MICKLETON HOOTER

Of all the Cotswold tales of dark deeds and the supernatural none is older or more mysterious than the legend of the Mickleton Hooter. When a person speaks of it he usually does so in a tone suggesting that the ultimate in ghostliness has been reached.

Yet ask that person to tell you what the Mickleton Hooter is and he will be hard put to give you an answer. Nor can the younger generation of Mickleton dwellers, who have grown up with the legend, tell you for sure what it is all about.

Perhaps this is not surprising for those few writers who have committed themselves to print about the Mickleton Hooter have been far from unanimous on the subject. Writing in 1923, J. Louis Beavir, said of the Mickleton Hooter: "It assumed many forms, sometimes merely an awful cry the like of which was never heard on sea or land; frequently it appeared like a calf running silently on the top of a low wall and at times changing into a tall white figure like a woman, which on being approached vanished."

On the other hand Ernest Belcher, in his book, "Rambles Among The Cotswolds", published in 1892, says: "All seem agreed that the Hooter was never to be seen. Unearthly yells, moanings and screechings have been heard though whether they proceeded from natural or supernatural causes is involved in obscurity." He concluded: "For many years past no human being has heard the Mickleton Hooter."

This assertion no longer applies today. "I have heard the Mickleton Hooter all right," says Mrs Annie Graynoth, who was born in the village and who will be 89 next February. "I have heard it just lately but I have never seen it. My father - he was a Hidcote born man - always said that years and years ago before his time they were out there hunting and there are sandpits up there though I don't know where they are, and a man and his horse got in and he said it's him that's hooting but you don't know and it's hard to say.

"It's a terrible sound. It's not like an owl. It's a different sound from an owl. If anyone didn't know about it and went up the hill to Hidcote at night it would terrify them to death. A lady comes here to see me - I knew her when she was a girl - and she lay in bed and heard it the other night: so did I so there must be something. It's like someone calling for help. I have never heard it in the day-time and I have never heard of anybody seeing it. When us older people tell the young people about it they laugh and say there's nothing of the sort."

Mrs Graynoth and friend are not the only persons to have heard strange sounds coming from the direction of Mickleton Wood though there may be a topographical explanation for this. The reputed haunt of the Hooter is a wooded valley which plunges steeply from the crest of the Cotswold escarpment, near Hidcote, to the fringe of Mickleton churchyard at the foot of the hill. This valley is so narrow and its sides so steep that it might conceivably act as a funnel, distorting or magnifying ordinary sounds like an owl's hoot or vixen's shriek, but this does not explain tales of an apparition.

Support for the legend of a mysterious calf, pursued but never captured, comes from another Mickleton resident, Frank Fairfax, who says: "One old saying is that it is a calf with a man's head which goes through Mickleton wood at midnight every night. It comes tearing across the Ebrington road, goes over the valley below Kiftsgate and then disappears up Clopton way. We have heard noises up there when we used to go stopping for the hunting but we never knew what they were."

The legend of a ghost calf is firmly rooted in British folk lore and reports of such a creature being seen have been recorded in several counties. Perhaps the Mickleton story is merely a survival of some forgotten cult or myth and has no basis whatsoever in fact. Yet though you rule out any possibility of an apparition and though you explain quite logically how the noises come to be made, when you are out there alone in that deep, narrow valley which even on the brightest summer day wears an aura of gloom and melancholy, it is not difficult to imagine strange things happening there.

1961

ROOM FOR READING

As a connoisseur of reading rooms I can say that the one at Evesham public library is a credit to the borough. It is better stocked than those at Worcester and Stratford-upon-Avon and easier to enjoy than the reading room at Oxford where a continuous game of basketball seems to be going on like thunder overhead.

All reading rooms appear to attract their quota of homeless wayfarers. You can't help feeling sorry for these flotsam who come inside for warmth and what they would probably call a kip but it is exasperating to find them snoozing over the latest copy of "Life" or "Illustrated London News" which you particularly want to read.

It might be a good idea for reading rooms to provide a number of empty magazine covers, appropriately labelled "The Snoring Times" or "Sleeping Gazette" behind which such patrons could slumber to their heart's content without depriving anyone of valuable reading matter.

It used to puzzle me a good deal why these vagrant types should prefer reading the "Daily Telegraph" to any other newspaper or periodical provided at Evesham reading room. Then the truth dawned! Before the layout of the reading room was changed this newspaper was located directly above the radiator!

All sorts of adventures can befall you even in such a humdrum place as a public reading room. Only a few weeks ago in the Evesham reading room I was startled to see a young man suddenly stop reading the "Daily Express" and hurtle to the floor as rigidly as a falling tree. I was ready to call for an ambulance since I assumed that even if his collapse were not serious he would certainly be suffering from the effects of his spectacular fall. But his companions assured me that he was all right and his behaviour not unexpected. Yes, he was the worse for drink and like most inebriates had fallen without causing himself the slightest injury.

But my oddest adventure occurred when I visited a public reading room not in the Four Shires area. I had just settled down with the "Illustrated London News" when a middle-aged man came hurrying over to me with a copy of that morning's "Telegraph" in his hand.

"Are you any good at crossword puzzles," he said. Like a fool I answered "Yes" and without waiting to be invited he sat down beside me. "Would you mind helping me with this one in the 'Telegraph'?" he said, adding reverentially, "There's a prize for it you know."

He ran his finger down the list of clues. "How about this one?" he said. "'Thirty-two across, a three letter word. The clue is 'For two bucks it could be a casus belli.'"

"'Casus belli' means a cause of war," he added. "I looked it up."

I told him the answer was "Doe."

"Why?" he asked.

"Because a doe is a female deer," I replied.

He looked puzzled. "But why should that be a cause of war?"

"Because during the mating season the bucks fight..." But here I paused. I had become aware that the other readers in the vicinity had lowered their magazines and were gazing at me, not with disapproval as one might have expected from the noise I was making but with fascinated interest.

I dropped my voice as low as I could. "Because the bucks fight..."

"Can't you speak up a bit," said my companion. "I'm a bit deaf you know."

"Because the bucks fight over the does in the mating season!" I exclaimed.

"But what are bucks?" came the inevitable reply.

This was too much for the man who had been reading "Motor Cycling" at the other end of the table. "They're male deer, you clot!" he bellowed.

Suddenly the light dawned. "You're a genius!" cried my companion, slapping me across the back. "Go to the top of the class!" Leaving me he hurried off to the other wide of the room where his cronies were sitting with their copies of the "Telegraph".

His voice came reverberating across the room. "Number thirty-two across is 'Doe'. He's working on the next clue now."

This was twenty-five down, a five letter word. The clue was: "It may be tickled to death without seeing the joke." I decided the answer must be "Trout."

"But why trout," asked my inquisitor when he rejoined me.

"Because that's the way you catch them - by tickling them," I explained.

This obviously did not register with him at all. "But why doesn't it see the joke?" he asked.

"Well you wouldn't think it was funny if you were a fish and you were being caught, would you?"

To see the light of comprehension flooding over the man's face was ample reward for all, the embarrassment I was enduring. "Wonderful!" he said. "You're a gem!" And off he went scampering across to his cronies. "Number twenty-five down is 'Trout'. Fill it in," he told them. "The next's on the way!"

Thus it went on till I had done as much as I could.

"I'm sorry, I can't do any more," I said apologetically, handing him back the newspaper.

"Never mind!" he said brightly. "You've done very well. I was lucky to come across you". And, ridiculously, I could not help feeling proud.

He went further up the room to an elderly gentleman reading the "Geographical Magazine." Are you any good at crossword puzzles?" he asked him.

1962

THE BALLOONS CAME DOWN

The fall-out of contestants from the balloon race from Oxford to Stratford-upon-Avon is the nearest the Cotswolds are likely to get to an invasion from Space at least for the time being. It was in the early evening that the first balloons began to appear like multicoloured Easter eggs floating in the sky. Then as the balloonists reached the Cotswold ridge things began to go badly wrong.

They were obviously losing height and jettisoning sand to retain altitude. Some of the sand landed on a postman's car at Moreton-in-Marsh. One gentlemanly pilot paused to salute a lady who waved to him with her handkerchief from her Moreton garden as his craft gently sank, a veritable captain going down with his ship.

Next a balloon piloted by a Dutchwoman came down at Longborough. Then a second landed on Aston Magna allotments, where one of the tenants was so intent on planting his runner beans that he completely failed to notice it. Another came down at Park Farm, Blockley, its trail rope catching an overhead power cable and cutting off the local electricity supply. The pilots, clearly Frenchmen, embraced each other and drank a toast in champagne.

Meanwhile the Dutchwoman was pedalling fiercely across country on a borrowed bicycle to report her whereabouts. A balloon that came down at Downs Farm, Blockley, narrowly missed some holly trees and the pilots, Germans, toasted their lucky escape with wine. A less sophisticated British Army couple in khaki lit up cigarettes when their craft safely but prematurely hit terra firma. Other balloons piloted by Germans and Americans made emergency landings near Broadway and Honeybourne.

Instead of being met with pitchforks and cudgels the balloonists were generally greeted warmly and with babies snatched out of bed by their parents to see the strange men who had fallen from the sky.

1965

GOOD CLEAN HORROR

An unfulfilled childhood wish has at last been granted: I have seen "The Bride Of Frankenstein". When the film first came to Evesham I was too young to see it because it had an H for Horrific certificate which meant that no-one under 16 was admitted.

But I wanted to see it desperately. On my way to and from the infants' school I used to gaze enviously into Alcock's window, where the stills from the film were on display. What they were doing in a music shop in High Street and not outside the cinema I cannot remember but that is where they were.

The "bride", who was wearing a shift of virginal white, had Marcel-waved hair which stood up on end as if it had an electric current running through it, which it probably did. As it had been assembled from the heads of different corpses the colour shade, ran the spectrum from silver through red to jet black.

Lunging towards her in what appeared to be an attempt at an embrace was the Monster himself with nuts and bolts holding his neck up and a livid red line on his forehead where the skin had been rather clumsily stitched together to secure his scalp.

It seemed to me the most intriguing romance since King Kong flipped at the sight of Fay Wray and climbed up the Empire State Building with her in his hand. I had not been able to see that film either, which also had an H certificate, but I had been deeply impressed by the giant cut-out which had the monster gorilla together with his screaming paramour climbing up the outside of the Clifton cinema or the Scala as it was then. Cinemas don't seem to go in for these sort of extravagances any more.

Well the film came and went and I thought I would never hear of it again but as I was walking in Port Street last week I was surprised to see that the Regal was reviving it as a supporting feature in their next programme. I was overjoyed. I was going to be able to beat the censor after all. Even the stills on display outside the cinema seemed to be those sepia-tinted originals that I had once seen in Alcock's window many years ago.

Unfortunately both the film and I are considerably older than we were then and if it were released for the first time today it would probably be given an H for Hilarious certificate. I cannot imagine the story horrifying anyone. It turns out that nobody can stand the sight of the Monster, which is understandable with all those bolts and stitches and things, and so Frankenstein, his creator, runs up an assembly job female to provide him with a companion of his own kind.

But you know what unpredictable creatures women are! When they unwrap the bandages from her and the female Monster takes her first look at her mate-to-be she can't stand the sight of him any more than anyone else and screams her head off as all the other females have done in the picture. The Monster, by now thoroughly fed up with always being the wallflower, blows himself, bride and mad doctor to bits by pulling on a conveniently situated lever.

They ought to have let me see the film when it first came out. I'm sure it wouldn't have done me any harm and it seems far less frightening than many of the things shown on television now.

For there was a sort of innocence about the horror films they made then. People got chucked over cliffs and clobbered on the head; mad doctors had pickled human brains in jars that looked more like sago pudding than anything else and monsters pulled funny faces but there was nothing basically nasty about it if you get what I mean. There wasn't the sick, self-indulgent horror that one comes across so often these days. It was all good clean fun.

1967

A LION ESCAPED

On a summer's day 65 years ago in 1897 a travelling circus came to Moreton-in-Marsh. It set up its tent in a field where the saleyard is now and boastfully advertised a twice-daily show which included a lion taming act.

The tent was full of children for the first performance on the Saturday afternoon. They sat crowded round the small arena laughing and chattering with excitement at this unexpected treat. Only one little girl called Ida Gray felt ill at ease. She was sitting in the back row nearest the exit, wishing that she was still at home. She had a premonition that the lion was going to escape.

In another part of the town, at Bengal House, Mrs Yelf, the local doctor's wife, was entertaining guests to tea in the garden of her home. They made a gracious picture, sitting on bamboo chairs on the broad lawn with the china laid out on a dainty cloth-covered table. Adjoining the garden were the doctor's stables, which contained two horses, a chestnut gelding and a black mare.

A little boy called Frank Dyer was visiting the stables to see his father, William Dyer, who was employed by Dr Yelf as a groom. His father was not there and after waiting for him for a while, the boy decided he had better go home or his mother would be cross with him for being late for tea. The time was 5.30pm.

In the circus tent the ringmaster was just announcing the lion tamer's performance which formed the grand finale of the show. There was an excited murmur as the lion tamer mounted the steps to a cage containing a lion which sat crouching in one corner. It was his intention to enter the cage...

As he opened it he signalled to a negro attendant to close the door immediately he was inside. The lion saw that his attention was momentarily diverted and seized its opportunity. It squeezed between the side of the door and the lion tamer's legs and leapt out into the crowded tent.

There were terrified screams as the lion knocked down several of the children near the cage and plunged through the scattering audience towards the entrance flap. As it reached the flap and disappeared out of the tent its long tail slashed across Ida Gray who sat there petrified with fright. Her nightmare had come true.

Having gained its freedom the lion bounded out of the field into a lane running beside the infants' school, which was closed for the week-end. It raced down the lane till it reached the main London road and crossed the highway into Dr Yelfs' drive".

As the lion entered the drive it met the little boy, Frank Dyer, who was running home as fast as he could and the two of them collided head-on. Fortunately the lion seemed almost as surprised at the encounter as the boy was and raced on without doing him any harm. It then slunk into the stables where it promptly received a kick in the ribs from the black mare.

The enraged lion jumped at the mare and brutally clawed is hind quarters but the gallant mare was more than a match for its opponent and drove it into an empty stall separating the mare from the gelding.

Meanwhile Mrs Yelf's tea party was rudely broken up by a posse of circus people and bystanders, who invaded the garden carrying a variety of sticks and makeshift weapons. However, the hostess and her guests were not sorry to retreat to the house when told there was an escaped lion in the vicinity. The animal was traced to the doctor's stable, where the door was shut fast to imprison it for the time being.

The problem remained of how to get the lion out of the stable and back into its cage. After several plans had been discussed, a portable hen house was borrowed and propped up against the stable door. A man climbed on top of the hen house with the sliding top raised in his hand ready to be lowered.

The lion tamer dropped into the stable through a skylight and proceeded to give the performance of his life, using not a whip or chair but a borrowed pitchfork. After several failures he persuaded the lion towards the stable door, which he had earlier opened. The animal ran out, the man on the hen house dropped the lid and the lion found itself ignominiously trapped in a hen coop.

A triumphant procession returned to the circus field bearing the hen house and its occupant shoulder high and the lion was returned to its cage just in time for the evening performance. Despite the afternoon's incident there was a packed house for the show.

What afterwards became of the characters in this story? Of the lion and its tamer nothing was heard after they had moved on from the district. The mare survived its brutal attack thanks to the gentle treatment administered by Dr Yelf and his groom, William Dyer. A number of people still alive today remember having seen the scars on the mare's rump when the doctor's carriage visited their streets or village.

Dr and Mrs Yelf, a much respected couple, lived in Moreton for many years but eventually retired to Church Norton in Hampshire where a stained glass window in the church was recently dedicated as a memorial to them and their son, who died tragically in an accident.

The little girl, Ida Gray, is now Mrs Arthur Drury, who lives at The Limes in High Street, Moreton, and is probably the last surviving member of that circus audience of 65 years ago still resident in the town. She says she has always avoided circuses since then. What of the little boy, Frank Dyer? Here our story takes on an ironic note. Having escaped possible death after colliding in the street with an escaped, angry lion he was to lose his life less than twenty years later fighting for his country in the First World War and his name is to be seen on the town's War Memorial to this day.

1962

ABNORMAL SERVICE

The station staff at Moreton-in-Marsh had a shock last week-end when the 5.35pm passenger train calling at Evesham, Moreton and Oxford went straight through the station without stopping. Passengers on the train wishing to alight at Moreton were dumbfounded and were eventually sent back an hour later on a special diesel train. It is understood the train failed to stop owing to a misunderstanding on the part if the driver.

1960

Rail passengers from Moreton to Oxford had a depressing experience during last week's cold spell. The 7.30am diesel train developed engine trouble almost immediately after leaving Moreton and took an hour and 10 minutes to do the seven mile journey to Kingham. It never actually stopped nor did it ever really get going. The station staff at Moreton watched bemused as the train took a full 20 minutes to disappear from view. At Kingham the train crept thankfully into a siding for attention. The trouble is understood to have been caused by excessive frost.

1982

Moreton station's most fashionable train - the 5.15pm out of Paddington on Fridays bringing the elite of the district into the Cotswolds for the week-end - ran into trouble last Friday when it ground to a halt about 200 yards short of the platform.

Knights, company directors, city financiers, past and present debutantes and mere students, faced with the problem of being so near and yet so far decided to complete the rest of the journey on foot. Numbering 63 in all they threaded their way along the track towards the platform where their baffled chauffeurs, whose gleaming cars turn Moreton's station yard into a miniature motor show on Fridays, gazed helplessly on.

The cause of the trouble was that an earlier diesel train had broken down and blocked the track.

1966

COUNTRY CALENDAR

Opening Aubrey Seymour's book, "Fragrant The Fertile Earth", is like inviting in an old friend - in this case a genial, sagacious countryman - and listening with enjoyment as he talks about things which interest him and which he thinks will interest you.

For his writing has the spontaneity and directness of person-to-person conversation. To read his book about life in the country generally and in his own corner of it in particular, is to feel that you have really been in his company for an hour or two.

It is a very personal book. Most of it concerns what he himself has seen, done or heard about first-hand, and with the art of a raconteur he manages to make it sound as though it is all specially addressed to you.

Unlike most conversation, however, the book has shape and discipline. Each of its chapters is devoted to a month of the year: like some illustrious predecessors Mr Seymour has written a Country Calendar. Nor is it discursive as some talkers can be. He knows when he has gone on long enough about a particular subject. He is never a bore.

His first chapter is on November with the explanation: "The conventional calendar ends with December but by the countryman's reckoning the year comes to a close when the crops are harvested and the flocks and herds brought down to their winter quarters. When the farmer had his say Halloween, the last day of October, saw the old year die and I propose to revert to the ancient tradition and begin my calendar of country life with November."

And each succeeding chapter is concerned with a month and the labours, pursuits and frivolities to be expected within its orbit. Each is prefaced by quotations which range from Shakespeare to Damon Runyon and the book is illustrated with delightful sketches all from the author's own hand.

And when the year is over and November has returned the impression left behind is of the timelessness of country life. Mr Seymour can talk of sickles and flails and in the same breath mention a combine harvester without the latter seeming an intruder. The country comfortably absorbs the new and moves inexorably on.

This mingling of time past and present is epitomised by the two endpapers: a plan of Weston Mill, near Shipston-on-Stour, where Mr Seymour lives, and a map of the Cotswold-Warwickshire border, which manage to look as though they had been drawn to illustrate Jane Austen or Thomas Hardy yet contain such observations as: "Stick of German bombs fell here."

In his introduction Mr Seymour says: "Leisure has been forced on me by circumstances that no man can escape unless he die young, and to what better use can I put it than in tracing the changing pattern of the year as I have observed it in the triple role of farmer, sportsman and naturalist?"

It is indeed something to be grateful for that old age should have provided the leisure for Mr Seymour, now in his eighties, to reveal unexpected talents as a writer and artist and something to marvel at that there should hare been such a late flowering.

1970

CAMP SONG

It was suggested at a meeting of Cheltenham District Council, whose area stretches into the Cotswolds and includes Winchcombe, Stanway, Stanton and Snowhill, that a special camping site be provided for gipsies to avoid any possibility of their becoming a nuisance.

"Oh where shall we camp tonight, Ma?
By the hedge where the pitchin' is dry
Or under the wood where the owls hoot
Till morning puts light in the sky?"

"No, Dad, we'll go to the camp ground
What the council have built in the lane,
With water on tap and a clothes line
And a thing where you pulls down the chain!"

1957

TALK ON A HILLTOP

The scene is the top of Langley Hill, near Winchcombe. An old man and a young man are standing side by side, gazing at the view. It is fairly late in the evening and the brilliant light of the setting sun illumines the landscape. From where they stand the two men look down on an unspoilt valley with the steep slopes of the Cotswold escarpment rising romantically all round it.

OLD MAN: Why have you come up here, young man?

YOUNG MAN: Because I want to see the view.

OLD MAN: It is certainly very beautiful.

YOUNG MAN: Then you had better make the most of it because it won't look like this much longer.

OLD MAN: What do you mean?

YOUNG MAN: The electricity board are building an overhead power line across here from Melksham in Wiltshire to Hams Hall in Warwickshire. The pylons will come from the direction of Cleeve Hill Common, pass between this hill and Prescott Hill and then go off towards the Washbournes and Ashton-under-Hill.

OLD MAN: Oh, well, I suppose it is all part of progress.

YOUNG MAN: Do you call that progress!

OLD MAN: Well, pylons aren't necessarily ugly things. Some people think they are beautiful in a modernistic way.

YOUNG MAN: Not these pylons! They are going to be like nothing you have ever seen before. They are to be 136 feet tall - that's 26 feet higher than Evesham bell tower - and all the trees have got to be cut down within 100 feet of them.

OLD MAN: But there's no need to look at the pylons. There will be plenty of unspoilt scenery around them.

YOUNG MAN: I don't call it a view if you have to wear blinkers to appreciate it.

OLD MAN: Well go somewhere else then. There are other beautiful places besides this one.

YOUNG MAN: That's where you're wrong. The number of unspoilt places in this country gets fewer every year. The same thing that is happening to this valley is happening to dozens of other valleys up and down the country. Britain will soon be criss-crossed with overhead wires and cables from Land's End to John o' Groats!

OLD MAN: (warming up): It's all very well for you to talk! You are a young man and take such things as electricity for granted. When I was a boy we had to make do with paraffin lamps and candles. We didn't have half the advantages that people living in the country take for granted today. If you had lived in those days you might feel differently about pylons.

YOUNG MAN: In other words, so long as you and your generation are comfortable it doesn't matter how we leave the country for future generations. When you were young, England was a green and pleasant land. Look at it today! Practically any kind of unsightly horror can be got away with in the name of progress.

OLD MAN: If this country doesn't progress there won't be any future generations to enjoy the country! We are an industrial nation and have got to keep up with modern developments and not let other countries beat us; These pylons will make all the difference to industry in the Midlands or wherever the electricity is intended for.

YOUNG MAN: They will also have to be paid for. Do you know that it is going to cost £30,000 per mile to build this power line? And with the rate we are developing atomic power it will probably be obsolete in ten years' time but then it will be too late. This part of the country which you said yourself was beautiful will have been spoilt for good.

OLD MAN: Well don't get so worked up about it. When you're as old as I am you'll realise that there are more important things than pylons to worry about.

YOUNG MAN (aside): Silly old fool!

OLD MAN: What was that?

YOUNG MAN: I said it's chilly and cool. It's also getting dark. Come on, old man, let's go home.

The two figures then disappear from the hilltop and only the dusk and silence remain.

1957

JEALOUSY AND PASSION

This is a tale of jealousy and passion, ending in stark tragedy. It begins last October when two swans flew out of the dull autumn sky and settled on the duck pond at Moreton-in-Marsh. They were obviously newly-mated and enjoying a first home of their own. The people of the town, exceedingly hospitable, fed them and encouraged them to stay. The pond had been untenanted for years and it was pleasing to see white wings on its dark water again. Nobody then imagined that the scene was being set for violence and death.

All went well for several weeks until Moreton-in-Marsh was flooded as a result of a rapid thaw at Christmas. The swans flew away and nothing was heard of them for a fortnight but just when it was feared they had gone never to return, the birds reappeared on the pond one morning just as though nothing had happened.

But something had happened: things were not as they had been before. The female was unsettled, nervous, always on the move, either making short flights to Mr Tarplett's field or going on longer journeys to who knows where? Some people predicted a blessed event was imminent. Alas! The explanation was not as innocent as this. Often the female would go, leaving her mate on his own until impatient with waiting he would go off looking for her and bring her back home. Who can say when he first suspected the truth, when he first realised that he was being deceived: that there was another swan? Yes, the female was being unfaithful to him. It was the eternal triangle all over again, this time on water.

Maybe she felt the same way about Moreton-in-Marsh duck pond that some of the townspeople do: that it is shabby and disgusting and not fit for a decent swan to be seen on. Maybe her mate kept telling her too many funny stories about when he was a cygnet or describing the delicious titbits his mother used to give him. At any rate the female was paying regular visits to her paramour out Adlestrop way. She was sometimes gone for days.

If the male did not understand before he was left in no doubt as to the situation when his mate and the other swan returned to the pond together. He was bound to regard this as a deliberate provocation as they had no doubt intended it to be. Obviously things could not go on as they were. The pond was not big enough to hold the three of them. One of the males would have to give way.

The horrible climax occurred last Sunday afternoon as the church bell was tolling. It was the only sound to be heard apart from the noise of traffic on the nearby Fosse Way. Suddenly the two males could tolerate each other's presence no longer. With wings flaring they confronted each other across the pond, then burst into attack. The pond foamed where they fought and white feathers showered the air. The female looked mutely on, daring to encourage neither protagonist in case the wrong bird won. Her mate, however, was no match for the interloper and was driven nearer and nearer the bank adjoining the main road.

Beaten and humiliated he flapped frantically from the pond into the road in search of sanctuary. In his anxiety he forget the Highway Code and looked neither right nor left. There was a sudden scream of brakes and in less than a second the hapless bird lay crushed and dead under the wheels of a car.

Today there are only two swans on the pond again. One has a bloodstain on his forehead, the other floats serenely along, utterly inscrutable, keeping her secrets to herself. Is she sad at losing her mate, now buried by courtesy of the local council, or does she rejoice at having gained another companion? We shall never know for who can explain the mystery that is the female?

1957

WISDOM MUST PAY

When Gloucestershire took over part of Worcestershire on April 1 it also inherited Wisdom Davis, his wife, two daughters and a son, a family of caravan dwellers who had been camping illegally on a grass verge near Broadway tower.

At Chipping Campden Magistrates' Court on Wednesday Mr Davis pleaded guilty to camping on the highway and was fined £1. The court was told that he had already been summoned for parking on the same piece of ground when it was still in Worcestershire and had been fined £2 by the Evesham Bench. "It is one of the things we have inherited," Insp Kenneth Golding told the court.

Mr Davis explained that he had not yet paid the £2 fine imposed at Evesham because he had no money.

When the Bench asked who would be entitled to be paid first, Evesham or Campden, the clerk, Henry Saunders, replied: "I'll try and beat them to it if I can."

Mr Davis was allowed a week in which to pay the Campden fine. As he was deaf the clerk shouted to him that if he did not pay he would have to go to prison.

In a letter which he handed to the court, Mr Davis said he had not been able to find anywhere to go. He would move as soon as he possibly could. The letter bore hope, however, that the problem might soon be solved. It bore a PS which said: "This won't happen again. Mrs Davis."

1965

EVIL CHERUB

I have never forgotten the first time I set eyes on that evil cherub, that travesty of infanthood. It was round about the shortest day of the year and I was staying with friends at Tredington, near Shipston-on-Stour. Marion, Natalie and I had decided to walk over during the afternoon to see a friend at Honington, the next village. The weather was inhospitable but we had spent so much time indoors that we felt a breath of air might do us good, damp and uninvigorating though it proved to be.

As we walked along our conversation echoed noisily on the silent air as though we were talking in an empty vault, and we found ourselves instinctively dropping our voices. The trees, the fields, the earth itself, seemed so hushed and dead that one could scarcely imagine them ever coming to life again.

The friend I have mentioned lived in a cottage adjoining Honington Hall and so we decided to take a short cut through the privately owned woods lying between the hall and the road. This proved a doleful, eerie experience. On that grey afternoon there was not a flicker of sunlight: the wood was filled with shadows and dampness oozed from the bare branches of the trees.

As we trod our way through the dead leaves the white statues of forgotten gods and goddesses rose suddenly from the undergrowth, shrugging off the weeds from their marble shoulders. In the dimness of the wood they looked like frozen phantoms, pathetic in their humbled, neglected state.

After calling on the friend, someone suggested - I don't remember who it was - that we visit the church, which squatted by the entrance gates to the hall, almost in the pocket of the great house. Though the light was already fading we thought we just had time to go inside, something that we were to regret ere long. The church was engulfed by tall trees, which gave it a gloomy aspect, especially at that time of the year, and it also proved to be an 18th century Classical building, which further put me off.

I believe that Classical churches belong to the busy streets of a town or city where their sooty domes elaborate the skyline and their cheerful gold and white interiors prove a relief from the drab streets. Such churches lose their urban assurance in the country and look uncomfortable in an empty, verdant scene. So I entered Honington church without elation. Marion started to read aloud from the lectern as was her wont while Natalie and I wandered round the darkening church.

It was then that I saw IT floating on the wall above my head and though 15 years have passed since that moment I can still feel the shock it gave me. First, my attention was drawn to a marble skull with a snake crawling out of it carved at the base of a wall memorial to one Joseph Townsend who died in 1763. I wondered why bygone sculptors should wish to remind us so vividly of the end that all flesh must come to or why the dead should boast to the living "This is as I am and as you shall be!"

On looking higher I saw that the centrepiece of the memorial was a weeping child.... but what a child! Its body bulged like a prizefighter's and its face expressed not gentle grief but scowling adult rage. Yet it was its head, its grotesque head, that caused the most alarm. It ballooned out like no normal child's head has ever done almost as though it were growing a second head at the back.

By this time I had been joined by my two companions who were as disturbed by the creature as I was. "Why on earth should anyone wish to depict a child like that?" asked Marion. This indeed was the ultimate horror. What sort of person was it who would portray the beauty of childhood so repellently?

The church suddenly seemed colder and darker. Glancing outside I saw that the day had gone and the face of night was pressing against the windows. "Let's go home," I said to the others, who needed no persuading and the three of us hurried off through the gloom till the reassuring lights of Tredington shone before us.

That night we sat round a cheerful fire roasting chestnuts and feeling glad to be safe and warm indoors but occasionally, when my eyes met theirs, I could see that my companions had not forgotten what we had seen and nor had I.

1962

SCHOOL WITH A GRIN ON ITS FACE

The lamentations have been loud and long over the demise of Chipping Campden Grammar School but no-one seems prepared, publicly at least, to shed a tear for the passing of Moreton-in-Marsh Secondary Modern School. (The two schools are to be amalgamated to form a Comprehensive).

Yet tears should fall because when the school goes a gale of adventure in local education will have blown itself out. Thanks to the exuberance and flair of its first headmaster, Mr Lock, the Moreton school became, one feels, exactly what the 1944 Education Act hoped that a secondary modern school would be.

It was not only an attractive alternative to a grammar school. It was a place where children, especially those not academically inclined, could be happy and feel they belonged. School-going became not just a question of ink, blotting paper and rulers, but of living.

Something marvellous always seemed to be happening at Moreton Secondary Modern. One year the children would be cultivating their own forestry plantation. Next year they would be building a Rolls Royce in which to go away on holiday. School it was, but it was never dull!

Looking back on those awful days when the children had to trudge from hut to hut, from one part of Moreton to another, for their lessons, one marvels at the *esprit de corps* that Mr Lock managed to inspire in his far-flung scholastic empire.

He did it, one imagines, by building up the children's self-respect. They wore a uniform, published their own magazine and had a school motto *Labore et Honore*. The school was divided into four houses, Bredon, Cotswold, Malvern and Cleeve. There were holidays abroad and annual speech days. A parents' association was formed. Such things are taken for granted today but 20 years ago they were still regarded as the prerogative of luckier brethren at grammar schools.

There was the school orchestra with its genial, bearded conductor. When one thinks of those wailing recorders, those scraping violins, one wants to laugh. Then one remembers the serious rapture on the players' faces and feels ashamed of oneself.

There was that performance of "Iolanthe", the happiest of all school shows in the Cotswolds, and the pantomime in which the little devils conscripted to hold up the scenery, let it go spectacularly during the grand finale! With "Iolanthe" it would have been so much easier for the staff to train one cast but they trained two so that as many children as possible would enjoy taking part in the show. It was this kind of spirit that made Moreton Secondary Modern memorable.

It was during Mr Babbage's time - he was the school's second headmaster - that the appearance of the school was smartened. A grassy quadrangle was sown and flower-beds planted. Even so, the disorderly amalgam of wooden huts and Victorian stone buildings must have seemed to the staff a far cry from the ideal school they had dreamed of in their college days. Yet many of them stayed and came to love the school. One was Mr Davies, who has been headmaster for the past year and has had the painful task of presiding over the liquidation of the school.

There was never enough room for the annual speech day which was usually held out-of-doors for this reason. A telephone call was put through to the meteorological office at Little Rissington RAF Station and if the weather report was favourable, tables and chairs were put outside. If the day was wet, as many as possible were seated in the dingy school hall. The remainder of the children sat in their classrooms and had speech day relayed to them by loudspeaker or - this was the sort of enterprising school it was! - transmitted by closed circuit television.

A funny thing happened at one speech day at which the prizes were presented by a chairman of the County Education Committee, who told the children that he had been very impressed by what he had seen at the school and that when he got hack to Gloucester he was going to tell his committee: "We have got to do something for those children at...at...at..." He had forgotten which school he was visiting!

In fact, the education committee did not do a great deal for the school which was understandable. What good was it, pouring money into a school that was doomed to die. Yet Moreton Secondary Modern will not stick in the mind as an unhappy or deprived school. On the contrary, most of us will remember it as the school that always had a grin on its face.

1965

ROAST BEEF

A group of men at Stow-on-the-Wold have formed themselves into a club with the sole object of meeting once a month to eat as much English roast beef as they can comfortably digest. The beef is served up cold because they say it tastes better that way.

The club was formed as a result of a friendly argument between customers at the Unicorn Hotel on the subject of the merits of

English beef. One of the customers, Mr Richardson, a local bank manager, suggested the proof was in the eating and that a beef dinner be held to settle the argument.

Mr Lea, the hotel proprietor, agreed to take charge of the arrangements and the first dinner, attended by a dozen people, was held a year ago. The English beef more than justified itself, the dinner was a success and similar functions have been held at the Unicorn regularly ever since. The last was attended by thirty people.

As soon as one dinner has been held Mr Lea buys another large sirloin ready for the next dinner and it hangs for several weeks in a cool place before being taken down and roasted. It then stands for 24 hours until it is cold. The meat is served with horse-radish sauce and beer in pewter tankards is available to those who want it. The club is strictly confined to men.

Mr Richardson says: "What with the war and rationing the young fellows of today have never eaten real beef. They don't know what it is! Imported beef can't compare with home-produced beef but the trouble with English beef is that it is cooked too soon after it has been killed. It wants to hang a bit. We let ours hang for at least three weeks before we roast it. We eat it cold because that is the real way to taste good beef. You want to have a slice from a great chunk of roast sirloin which hasn't been touched until it has gone cold. My God! It's lovely!"

Only a few evenings ago Moreton-in-Marsh farmers proved to the nation by a simple experiment that English beef is better because it shrinks less in cooking than imported meat. They want English beef to be supplied to schools, hospitals and other places where good quality meat is essential. It could be that our Cotswold yeomen are paving the way to a nation-wide revival of the traditional cult of beef-eating!

1957

A COTSWOLD MONET?

The picture immediately seemed familiar. Not the picture itself but the scene it depicted, a quiet country road with a distinctive clump of trees on the left-hand side and not a person or building in sight. I was visiting Moreton-in-Marsh branch library, open all day Tuesdays and Thursdays, half day on Fridays and Saturdays, and after changing my book was browsing in its single shelf arts section. I had pulled out a thickish book with many illustrations called "History Of Impressionism" by John Rewald, director of the Metropolitan Museum in New York and a world expert on 19th century French Impressionist painting of which his museum has a supreme collection. The picture occupied a full page and was by Claud Oscar Monet, 1840 - 1926, the founding father of Impressionism, and I was sure I'd seen that road and those trees before.

I borrowed the book to take home and study further, hoping to work out where the location was, then suddenly the penny dropped: it was of course the road out of Upper Swell, a small village a mile from Stow-on-the-Wold which I had travelled through innumerable times. I got out the car and drove over there forthwith, stood with book in hand where I imagined the painter had stood, gazed at the picture and the scene beyond and found them to be identical though the road looked quieter in the painting than it was now. With a feeling of awe I realised I had made a momentous discovery! Monet had painted many pictures in London but was not known to have painted elsewhere in this country. I now knew him to have been in the Cotswolds. The evidence was there before my eyes.

I thought how wonderful it would be for the *Journal* to be able to publish two pictures side by side, one of the painting, the other of the scene as it looked today, and when I got home I flicked through the index at the back of the book to see who the picture belonged to. Inevitably it proved to be in a private collection in the United States, which made my chances of getting hold of a photo remote in every sense of the word.

However, nothing ventured, nothing gained, as the saying goes, and I sat down and wrote a letter to the owner explaining who I was, what I had discovered and asking whether I could borrow a photo of the painting for use in the newspaper which I promised - fingers crossed! - to return safely to him. (Papers are not altogether trustworthy in this respect!) I didn't really expect a reply. For one thing I only had the name of the town to go on and doubted whether an inadequately addressed letter would ever reach him. I was about as low on the journalistic ladder as it was possible to get nor was the *Journal* likely to be known outside the Four Shires let alone in America. Yet a reply I got and it came with a London postmark and contained amazing news.

It was from the owner's widow, living in London, who wrote in her own hand: "Your letter has been forwarded to me and I have just returned from the South of France and will be at the above address until the 30th of October. The Monet is here and I am willing to have you publish it providing you don't mention my name and the whereabouts of the painting." I was not only going to get a photo of the painting. I was going to be able to see the darned thing!

I made an appointment to visit the lady's residence and travelled by train to Paddington, arriving there in the early evening just as the sun was setting and the lights were coming on, the most magical hour of the day in the big city. Her apartment was in mansions overlooking Hyde Park and I presented myself at the office of the uniformed doorkeeper who after satisfying himself of my credentials and purpose of visit showed me into a lift and sent me up to the appropriate floor. I stepped out into a long corridor and was surprised how quiet it all was and the carpet was so thick that it felt like walking on sand. I pressed the bell button on the door which was immediately opened by a Filipino houseboy in a white jacket who had obviously been expecting me.

Without saying a word he led me into a drawing room which was crammed with lovely things, rather like those old photos of rich Victorian interiors. There were many paintings on the walls and soon I was standing in front of the one I had come to see, the Monet, the last thing I expected to happen when I first saw a reproduction of it in a book at Moreton-in-Marsh library. I must confess I was a bit disappointed by it. Obviously an early work it seemed to lack the sparkle that Monet's paintings usually have; that feeling of open air and light glinting on foliage, but at least I was there, seeing it for myself, and on the shelf below was that most desirable of objects, a photo of it for me to borrow for the paper. I saw nothing of my kind hostess who was presumably in her boudoir preparing for a glamorous night on the town. The important thing was that I was able to return home with the photo in my possession.

It appeared in the following week's paper next to a photo taken by our staff photographer of the site today so that the two could be compared. I doubt whether the *Journal* readers were much interested in what a dead painter had done or not done: they would be more interested in the hatches, matches and despatches in our personal columns and the local footballing results, but my reporter colleagues were deeply impressed, something that gave me pride at the time but embarrassment later on.

Early in 1973 the Arts Council put on an exhibition called "The Impressionists in London" in the Hayward Gallery, and when I went I found it had been padded out with paintings of other places in Britain by Impressionists, including Sisley's views of Wales and Renoir's work in the Channel Islands. The Monet was not included. And so I wrote to a reviewer of the exhibition, later to become the equal of Rewald as an Impressionist pundit, asking somewhat presumptuously, why the Monet had been left out and enclosing a copy of my article.

He wrote back saying he would very much like to see the picture to which I replied that I had been sworn to secrecy by the owner but if he cared to send me a sealed letter I would forward it on. This he and I did and I later got a letter from him thanking me for my help and saying that the owner had been extremely friendly and helpful. He had now seen the painting about which he had doubts as to whether it was by Monet. "It is certainly quite a powerful painting," he wrote, "but there were many things about it which just didn't fit with what I've seen of Monet's work at that period. On the other hand the Pissarros, Degas and Renoirs were fine. My conclusions are particularly embarrassing as it has been authenticated by Rewald in "History Of Impressionism", and he is not the sort of authority one challenges lightly."

Later Mr Rewald seemed to help solve the problem himself by omitting the painting from the next edition of "History Of Impressionism", a popular book that went through several editions. Indeed it had the reputation of being the book most stolen from art libraries. The copy at Moreton-in-Marsh library survived apart from having the Monet picture ripped out shortly after my article appeared and the distinctive clump of trees it depicted was soon chopped down either by coincidence or design. So it looked as though my Monet may not have been a Monet after all. Alas!

1973

MILLENNIUM EVE

The village church at Bourton-on-the-Hill was floodlit for the first time shortly after five o'clock in the evening on Friday, December 31, 1999, only a few hours before the commencement of a new year, a new century and the new millennium to commemorate which the lights had been installed. It is difficult to convey the excitement there was in the country - and indeed the whole world - on that night as these momentous events unfolded. We felt fortunate to be of a generation that could experience something that would not happen again for another thousand years.

Even so the number of people who turned up for the switching on of the lights came as a surprise: the church soon filled with parishioners of all ages from veterans who had spent all their lives locally to small children whose lives belonged to the century to come. Some people had to stand. It was whispered there would not be enough wine glasses to go round for the celebration after the service.

The inside of the building shone white against the darkness peering through the windows while flowers and greenery lingered on niche and pillar from the Christmas festival and a nativity crib stood under the chancel arch. Having managed to find places for ourselves, comfortable or otherwise, we were then told by the rector, Geoffrey Neale, to get up again and go outside for the lighting-up ceremony to be performed by Michael Gaden, whose parents kept the village pub, the Horse and Groom, and who had himself been a member of the parish council for 40 years.

With his six-foot plus figure looming in the porchway he told the congregation, now stumbling in the dark among the graves of their forbears, that he felt honoured to have been asked to pull the switch, adding that he hoped it was going to work. It did. A soft golden light crept over the building with the shadow of a cross from a finial being cast large against the tower wall for all to see. Though the weather was dry and not at all cold the night was dark with no moon or star to be seen, only the twinkling of the lights of Moreton-in-Marsh in the near distance. Yet no-one stumbled in the dark now. The churchyard filled with light as the power of the floodlighting grew and St Lawrence's looked like a golden ship sailing through the night.

On returning inside the church everyone was presented with a small candle to take up to the chancel for it to be lighted and placed on a tall wooden frame with all the others to form a dazzling cross which dominated the church. Mr Neale said the cross represented the light of God which would guide us through the new century. After the singing of the hymn, "All people that on earth do dwell", he said he had to cut and run because he had a similar sort of service to conduct in his other parish of Blockley literally in a few minutes' time and so he missed the glass of wine and mince pie that the rest of us enjoyed before returning outside to see the planting of a commemorative yew tree.

This was performed by Mrs Neen Holder, the oldest resident of the village, and Jack Weaver, the youngest whose first birthday was in a day or two's time. She was given a real spade but Jack had to make do with a toy one, which he wielded with the expertise one would expect from a farmer's son though he fell on his bottom more than once. With people living longer one wondered whether he or any of the other children present might still be around in a century's time to recall the night on which the tree was planted.

Before walking home, pausing now and then to admire the church in all its golden glory from a variety of angles, the members of the congregation autographed a large sheet of paper which was to be stored or framed and hung as a memento of their presence at a village occasion quite unforgettable in its simple way. Not many hours later we would wake on the first Sunday of the new century and new millennium to hear the bells of Bourton-on-the-Hill church broadcast on national radio at six o'clock in the morning, an unexpected cause for pride. The tower was still all aglow as its bells rang out in homes all over the kingdom, a symbol of past and present and beacon for the future.

1999

THE BUS SHELTER GUEST

A young man to this district came
Fatigued and sick in mind:
Full many a Cotswold mile he walked
But shelter could not find.

Then he beheld a wooden bench
In the shelter where we wait
To catch the bus, and went inside
To sleep for it was late.

Next morning villagers awoke
To find him still at rest
And wondered what they ought to do
With their bus shelter guest.

Police were asked if they would help:
They said, "What's all the fuss?
He's done no harm to anyone,
It's naught to do with us."

The Social Services were called
But answered, "No can do!
Whatever happens to this man
Is strictly up to you!"

Christmas was near: the village thought
Of Jesus in the stable
And said "We ought to help this man
As far as we are able."

They gave him food, they gave him drink,
Fresh clothing and a shower,
With folk around who cared for him
He strengthened by the hour.

Five days he dwelt where buses stop
To go home was his prayer:
Well-wishers put him on the train
And also paid his fare.

By Christmas he was home again
His family to thrill:
Jesus was there that Christmas time
At Bourton-on-the-Hill!

2000

GUN TOTIN' TOTS

Ian, aged five, wanted a toy gun for Christmas. Would I get him one? Nothing could be easier, I thought....till I reached the shop counter at Stratford-upon-Avon. What sort of gun did I want? asked the shop assistant. Did I want a twin-holster set with two "peace-maker" pistols? Or would I prefer a spring-release, break-open action 100-shot repeater? Also available at the same price, she added, was an automatic, front-feed, 100-shot repeater. And if I cared to pay a little more I could have a revolving chamber, spring-loaded catch, 100-shot repeater with "exquisite" engraving, attractive butts and break-open action.

Or perhaps I was more interested in the heavier stuff? For example there was a bolt-action, shell-ejecting rifle with telescopic sight and precision two-power lens. Or an FH rifle with plastic safety bullets, nine-shot magazine and "flexible" bayonet. Honestly, I was shocked. I have never come across a more comprehensive or terrifying armoury. Talk about the Campaign for Nuclear Disarmament! What we need is a Campaign for the Disarmament of Tiny Tots!

1962

SUNDAY REFUGE

Going to the pictures on a Sunday is a doleful experience. The cinema is packed with young people whose average age is about 18 and the films shown are not usually up to much. Indeed it would be useless showing good films because the audience is not particularly interested in what is happening on the screen. They strike you as being more like refugees from the outside world than interested filmgoers. It makes you wonder whether it might not do just as well to provide a warm cinema, play some music, go round with the popcorn occasionally and not bother to show a film at all.

Some of the programmes would certainly not be missed! Last Sunday for example local cinemagoers had the following wholesome selection to choose from: The Wild And The Willing (X), The Primitives, Corridors Of Blood (X), Nights Of Rasputin (X), Bachelor Party (X), Four Skulls Of Jonathan Drake (X), The Spider (X), The Brain Eaters (X), Gun Duel At Durango and Four Steps To Danger. Whatever happened to keeping the Sabbath holy?

1962

GOING INTO HOSPITAL

It happened on Bonfire Night, Thursday, November 5, 1992, at 7pm. I had to leave home early that day and missed going to the lavatory as usual after breakfast. When I went that evening after returning home the results were horrendous. The movement was jet black, there was black blood all over the place and the stench was appalling. The same thing happened the next morning before I set off to see my doctor who had no difficulty in identifying more black blood and said he would make an appointment for me to see a specialist at the local hospital. I had been in perfect health previously.

Fortunately Fate was on my side and a chance meeting quite possibly saved my life. That same day I happened to call on a friend who had a visitor, a relative, who was a nursing sister in charge of the endoscopy unit at a hospital some distance away and who became concerned when she heard what had happened to me. She said she would tell her boss about it when she returned on duty the next morning. On the Saturday my bowel movement was as bad as ever but on the Sunday it was improving and by Monday things were back to normal again making me feel the worst was over. Nothing like it had ever happened to me before.

A week later I received a call from the nurse's hospital asking me to go in the next day for two nights to undergo tests to include an endoscopy via the throat and a colonoscopy via my back end. She had put in a good word for me with her specialist boss and though I was obviously recovered I did what they said and tried to be a model patient while I was there in order not to let her down. After another week I had a second call from them telling me to come in the next day for major surgery. Having always been terrified of the surgeon's knife I made all sort of excuses not to go, explaining that everything was all right now and I was feeling fine but they insisted I go in immediately despite my protestations. Having heard nothing from my local hospital after four weeks about seeing a specialist I telephoned my doctor to tell him of the request I had received from the other hospital and though surprised at the way things had developed since I last saw him, he said I ought to do what they were asking and I went in on Tuesday, December 8, and underwent an operation the following day during which a section of my colon was removed. It was barely a month since the blood first appeared.

My stay in hospital was one of the most extraordinary experiences of my life. Each night we were kept awake by awful animal-like shrieks from nearby, not the sort of thing one expects to have to put up with in a recovery ward but when we complained nobody took any notice and the shrieking continued nightly. The nurses, usually so caring, were completely unsympathetic towards us and said it was only George. Towards the end of my stay they brought George into the ward, a stunted severely handicapped youth with a radiant smile who seemed overjoyed to meet us, his new friends, and we all felt ashamed and guilty about having complained.

A feckless couple took over the bed nearest the door, he a young man with kidney trouble and she his girl friend who spent most of the day visiting him. With the bed curtains drawn they were often suspected of being on the job, as my ward mates put it, and on one occasion they carried on so late that she missed the last bus home and had to telephone for a taxi at midnight.

On another occasion she left it too late to get anything to eat and 'phoned for a pizza to be delivered to the hospital, the mouth-watering fragrance of which was a torment to the rest of us, especially myself, a nil-by-mouth patient just yearning for solid food. Their greatest *coup* occurred when she managed to get hold of a wheelchair and whisked him off in his dressing gown and pyjamas to the nearest pub from which they were recaptured later by hospital staff.

The biggest bust-up between parents I have ever seen happened when a Sixth Former was brought in as an emergency case for an immediate colostomy. The father was dead against it saying that wearing a bag would ruin his son's chances of ever leading a normal life again. His mother said they must do what the surgeon wanted and they went at it hammer-and-tongs with the lad prostrate in bed between them until the father stormed out of the ward not to return. The mother then gave consent for the operation to proceed and afterwards the boy kindly allowed me to see the result of the colostomy, which I had previously feared might have also been my lot. The first thing I did after coming round after the operation was to grope to feel whether I had got a bag and was much relieved when I hadn't.

At no time did I suffer any pain except afterwards when I coughed or sneezed, which had an agonising effect on my incision and its stitches. The man in the bed next to mine was, I learnt, a pillar of the local church and looked it, being tall and stately with a benign expression on his face and a silver tonsure above it. His vicar used to call to see him most days and would kneel by the bed while they prayed together. One evening while they were at their orisons I gave a sudden almighty sneeze and as the pain hit me, loudly shrieked, "Oh, Christ!", not an expression I would normally use and one that would have been better avoided at that particular time and place! The biggest pain of the lot was when they yanked out my catheter tube but this time I managed to scream without blaspheming.

An elderly man came into the ward on the same day as I did for a simple operation on his rectum and was told he would only be in for a couple of nights but afterwards his waterworks refused to function and when I left after ten days he was still there. I felt so sorry for him. Each day the surgeon would come marching in on his rounds and get more and more impatient as the man's condition showed no signs of improving while he beamed on me like a headmaster with his star pupil as I made a copybook recovery and was allowed to go home two days earlier than expected.

Later I returned to the hospital for a liver scan conducted by an amiable man who told me afterwards: "I shouldn't be saying this. The doctor should be first to tell you. But I thought it might take a weight off your mind. There's nothing there. You're in the clear". My reaction must have been a disappointment to him because I didn't know what he was on about and failed to enthuse or clap my hands in the air. After a month I returned for my first check-up with the surgeon who broke the news at last that I had been suffering from cancer of the colon, which came as a shock though he assured me it hadn't spread to the liver and they had caught it in time and he was confident I would make a complete recovery, which I did.

I used to think that cancer sufferers must know what it is they've got. Now I'm not so sure. What I am sure of is that after this experience the days seem more precious than they did before and my life in the Cotswolds all the sweeter.

1992

The Trip Back

On a fictional Wednesday in Worcestershire 1950s

Patients win aid to sue for horrors of LSD therapy

by Rachel Sylvester

SIXTY NHS patients who were prescribed the hallucinogenic drug LSD by doctors as part of treatment for mental illness have won legal aid to sue for compensation.

The claimants were given the drug by about 15 hospitals from the 1950s to the 1970s. They have suffered long-term psychotic side effects including flashbacks, panic attacks, memory loss and, in one case, epilepsy.

During the 20-year period LSD was used to treat thousands of patients for depression, mental illness and alcoholism. Even patients with temporary and transient post-natal depression were often prescribed the drug.

The patients were told that LSD would open up their emotions and allow them to confront their fears.

But Ed Myers, a solicitor with the Manchester firm Alexander Harris, which is co-ordinating the action, says hospitals' "irresponsibility" led many patients to suffer horrific experiences.

"Our case will be that the clinicians knew of the side-effects but did not advise their patients of them, and the doses of the drug were too large and too frequent."

LSD was first prescribed by British psychiatrists in 1953. It was used by 74 doctors nationwide as an "access drug". Mr Myers said: "They would use LSD in the same way as a surgeon uses a scalpel — to open the patient up and find out what was happening inside.

"It was believed that the drug would reduce the patient to a primitive state and allow them to convey their innermost feelings."

But although hippy recreational users discovered the drug's dangers in the 1960s and its general use was banned in 1966, the side-effects of medical users were never monitored.

Dr John Henry, of Guy's Hospital poisons unit, said the risks were particularly high for depressive patients. "LSD is not a pleasant,

THE SUNDAY TELEGRAPH

DECEMBER 3, 1995

Evening News, January 12, 1995

Trip into unknown

▶ LSD stands for Lysergic acid diethylamide and is a man-made drug.
▶ It is derived from a fungus called ergot and is now an illegal Class A drug.
▶ In the 1960s it became the preferred drug of the growing hippy culture.
▶ LSD use has also been explored for its possible military and medical uses and experiments were carried out by the CIA in America.
▶ LSD was also used by psychiatrists who believed it may hold the key to solving a wide range of mental illnesses.
▶ The drug produces vivid, sometimes terrifying hallucinations, but there is no evidence that it is physically addictive.
▶ Prolonged use can cause long-term damage to the nerve endings of the brain causing spontaneous acid trips or "flashbacks."

LSD guinea pigs win their right to legal aid

FORMER patients of Powick Hospital, near Malvern, who were given LSD during the 1960s have won legal aid to claim damages.

Last year the Evening News revealed that around 700 people suffering from mental illness had been treated with LSD at the hospital.

Many claim the drug aggravated their mental disorders and left them suffering anxiety, paranoia and flashbacks.

At the time, Powick was seen as the centre of experimental use of LSD in the 1950s, '60s and '70s in Britain under the guidance of the late Dr Arthur Spencer.

Mr Ed Myers, the solicitor acting on behalf of some of the patients in what is believed to be the first such claim involving the drug, said the granting of legal aid was a "big step forward."

He will now have to trawl through medical records to find out whether doctors used correct medical procedure and if proper monitoring took place.

---

given LSD in 1957 after a nervous breakdown, says he developed epilepsy as a result. "The sensation when I get an epileptic attack is very similar to some of the feelings when I was given LSD," he said.

"I see huge spiders crawling across the carpet or, if someone puts a hand on my shoulder, it will turn into a terrifying monster's hand."

Many of the claims are against the West Midlands Health Authority, whose Powick Mental Hospital administered LSD to at least 700 people in a special unit. Ken Purchase, the local Labour MP, is pursuing compensation on behalf of many LSD victims.

Ex-patient tells of Powick LSD 'flashbacks'

by NICK WATSON
Evening News

1. MORNING

Noise. The laughter of children in the street outside. Light. A shaft of sunlight cutting across the darkened bedroom through a gap in the curtains. Martin heard the noise, then felt the light worrying his shut eyelids, and as his mind began stirring he realised he was waking up and tried hard to prevent it. The world he was leaving was warm and safe, that to which he was returning was somehow frightening and dangerous. Anxiously he tried to tie up the broken ends of sleep but it was no use: the more he struggled, the more alert he became until he lay wide awake on the pillow; and as he opened his eyes he remembered it was Wednesday, the pounding in his head started up again and his limbs began trembling. The fear that he had shaken off the night before on sleeping was reawakening with him.

How could he get through another Wednesday? His body felt too limp for him to be able to lift himself from the bed. It was as though invisible plugs had been removed from his arms and legs and all the strength was draining from him. A tide of heat swept over his body and for a moment his skin felt too raw to bear the touch of the sheets, then he was cold and trembling again and all the time his head pounded and that voice inside kept repeating that these were the symptoms of madness, that he was going out of his mind.

He pulled himself upright as if to escape from the voice and felt suddenly calmer as he recognised the familiar objects round the room: the framed Bible texts on the walls, the bedside clock, his clothes on a chair and the washbasin with a tumbler containing his toothpaste and brush on a shelf. Even the wallpaper with its gaudy posturing flowers seemed a reassurance. Slowly his fear was replaced by a soothing optimism that reinvigorated his arms and legs, and though the voice in his brain persisted he could answer it back now.

"The bad feeling is passing," he could say, "and I am all right. Not paralysed. Not crazy." It might answer that this was Wednesday but he knew this would be the last Wednesday. There would be no more Wednesdays to wake up to like this one.

He got out of bed, went over to the window and drew back the curtains. The sunlight had that exaggerated brilliance that does not last for long when it comes early in the morning: by ten o'clock it would be dull again, possibly even raining. Chalked on the road's surface was a hopscotch circle and it was here that the children were playing, jumping from number to number and laughing or shouting as they landed on a wrong square and had to go back to the beginning again. They were making the most of the sun before setting off for school. A woman was already on the doorstep of one of the houses calling her child home.

Not long ago he had been one of those children playing in the street, unconcerned about what day of the week it was or what the day had in store. This was his street, the neighbourhood into which he had been born eighteen years before and from which, like them, he had once set off each morning on the reluctant walk to school. Its brick terraces with their grey slated roofs and scrubbed doorsteps were the backcloth against which he had grown up and within their walls lived people he had known all his life. Martin knew that what he had been doing these past weeks amounted to a betrayal of their trust, a breaking of the pattern of ordinariness with which a resident of the street was expected to conform in order to be acceptable to his neighbours, and that if they found out what he had done things would never be the same again.

It was true that he wanted nothing more now than to slip back into the pattern and be the same as he had been before and if he acted decisively today there was a chance he would get away with it. It was entirely up to him. That voice in his head, always ready to wear him down, might argue that he would not succeed, that his nerve would fail or something would go wrong, but Martin knew that he must not allow himself to be demoralised by it with the day hardly begun and he with so far to go. Forsaking the window, he crossed quickly to the washbasin, turned on the hot water tap and tried suppressing the voice in the business of getting himself washed and dressed.

He lathered his face and began shaving, a ritual that he looked forward to because he felt as relaxed then as at any time during the day. Using the razor required such concentration that other thoughts went from his mind and all that mattered was the stroke of the blade on his chin and the pleasant steamy warmth rising from the basin.

When he had finished he wiped his face with a towel and looked in the mirror to see whether he had left traces of soap behind. It still came as something of a surprise that his features should be so unchanged. His appearance was no different now from what it had been a couple of months ago, the face no whiter, hollower or more perturbed. His uncombed sandy hair, still untidy from sleep, hung over his forehead reaching the darker eyebrows, under which the grey eyes looked quietly back at their reflection in the glass. Perhaps there were shadows and a tautness of the skin around the eyes that had not been there before though no-one but himself would be likely to notice. Mrs Maling had said nothing and she would be the first to comment, which reminded him that she would be expecting him down to breakfast soon and did not like to be kept waiting with a meal on the table. His usual time for going downstairs was quarter-past-eight and as he strapped on his wristwatch he saw he had about five minutes to go, time enough in which to slip on his clothes and run a comb through his hair. It was while he was dressing that he heard a cry coming from the street, not immediately outside but some distance off. At first he could not tell what it was but as it grew nearer he recognised the sound. "Rag-a-boon!" it went. "Rag-a-boon!"

Putting on his jacket he returned to the window and looked into the street again. The sky was already dulling over and the sunlight came only spasmodically now. The children had all gone indoors except for one small boy still hopping around the chalk circle, a school cap jammed on his head. As he hopped from square to square his woollen stockings kept sinking to his ankles, causing him to have to stop from time to time to pull them up again.

The Trip Back

Coming down the middle of the street was the author of the cry, the town's ancient rag-and-bone man, a dilapidated figure with a long overcoat hanging almost to his feet and tied round his waist with a piece of string. A dirty trilby hat was pulled over his head. On his hands were mittens through which his black-nailed fingers clutched at his pram, which wobbled along not one of its bent wheels rotating in quite the same direction as the others. "Rag-a-boon!" he wailed. "Rag-a-boon!"

His eyes were hidden under the shadow cast over his upper face by the brim of his hat but a little glitter shone from the darkness occasionally as he glanced around him. His chin was covered with black whiskers while above his mouth hung an unkempt moustache. His nose stuck out sharply but his mouth beneath, lacking teeth, appeared to have caved in. All that was left was a crease that widened as he emitted his call, "Rag-a-boon!" His progress was slow because he had a bad leg, which he dragged sideways, and his pram at this early hour was empty, no housewives having yet taken out to him the rags and bottles and other junk he sought. He cut a grotesque figure but having walked the streets for so many years was accepted as a sort of local institution though times had changed and he could not have made much of a living. It was almost as though he felt he had to keep wandering the streets because it was expected of him.

If the boy in the road saw the man with the pram approaching he showed no sign of it. He was intent on mastering the hopscotch so that he could beat the other children in the afternoon after school: that is, provided the chalk marks had not been washed away by the now almost inevitable rain. Nor did he show any interest when his mother, a thick-armed woman wearing an apron, came out of the houses and shouted to him to come home. He simply went on hopping as though he had heard nothing. The woman's chest rose as she raised her voice to warn him of the consequences of his disobedience.

Still the boy took no notice. He was determined to delay his departure for school as long as he could: besides he knew from past experience that he was too nimble for his overweight mother to catch him. The woman appreciated the disadvantage but was reluctant to be beaten by the child, especially in front of neighbours who might be watching from behind twitching curtains. "Come on, there's a good boy!" she cried in a more conciliatory tone but this appeal had no more effect on the boy than the others had done.

It was then that the embarrassed woman became aware of the approaching rag-and-bone man and realised that she might have found a fortuitous ally in persuading her disobedient son to behave. She raised her voice again. "The rag-and-bone man's coming!" she shouted. "You know what he does to naughty boys!"

"Yes," thought Martin at his bedroom window. "I know," and looked to see what effect the woman's words would have on the child.

The boy had stopped hopping now and was facing up the road in the direction from which the pram was coming. His body had gone still but he kept his legs apart, apparently determined to stand his ground. "I don't care!"' he shouted. "I'm not afraid of him!" At least his mother now had the satisfaction of a reply and of seeing him stop his game.

The rag-and-bone man came slowly down the street with the pram wheels making a sinister squeaking, the only noise to be heard at that moment in the quiet street. He stared at the boy from the darkness beneath his hat and the boy, not moving, stared back though he looked nervous now and his legs seemed to be shaking a little. At last the rag and-bone man drew close enough for his black shadow to seep across the road and touch the boy's feet.

"Hallo, sonny," he said softly. "Are you a good boy? Or are you one of them bad boys I takes along with me?"

At this the boy's resistance vanished. He turned and ran, his feet flying across the street till he had reached his mother and put her ample presence between himself and the figure in the road. "Tell him to go away!" he shouted. "I don't like him!" Though expecting the child's reaction and welcoming it, the woman was nevertheless startled by the suddenness and intensity of it but soon recovered to turn the situation to her advantage. "You should have come when I first called you," she said. "That's why he came along the street - because you was naughty" and the two of them disappeared hand in hand indoors.

The Trip Back

The rag-and-bone man stood in the road making a wheezing noise that was his version of laughter. The crease in his face opened dark and wide, his shoulders were shaking and he let go of the pram once or twice to clap his hands. He was aware of his power to frighten small children and did what he could to promote it as a means of self-protection. When the boys were older they would plague him with their mimicry, horseplay and abuse; for a while, at least, he would keep them at bay by terrorising them as one day they would try to terrorise him.

Martin remembered how frightened he had been of the man with the pram and how is own parents had invoked the image of the rag-and-bone man to make him behave as a boy. The legend among the small children, which the older boys and even the parents did nothing to refute, was that the rag-and-bone man, who liked to be given things, prized children above all and that when they misbehaved would take them away in his pram and sell them to the butcher. Even now Martin winced at the thought of his body hanging from a hook in some shop window, then he glanced at the pathetic, lopsided old man in the street and smiled. How absurd that he and several generations of children should have been taken in by such a story!

His smile went when he looked at his watch and saw that it was some minutes past a quarter-to-eight. In watching the little drama outside he had forgotten the time and inadvertently committed the sin of being late for breakfast. He quickly combed his hair and went to the door but before leaving, turned for a last look at his room. By the time he saw it again that evening Wednesday would be over and there would be nothing more to fear but before then the day would have to be got through and he prayed for it to go quickly and successfully. If he was to break with them, as he must, he would have to be strong and this was something that he had never been with other people. He always lost, always gave in, and that voice in his head told him that he was going to do so again, but Martin knew that this time he really had no choice. To stand firm was on this occasion the only option.

Mrs Maling was already sitting at the breakfast table when he arrived downstairs. The table was a large round one with a permanent pile of cumbersome silver cruets in the centre. These were for show and a small plastic set was brought out of the sideboard for everyday use. Adjacent to the table was this sideboard, a bulging mahogany construction, and these two large pieces of furniture almost filled the small room. Lace curtains at the window obscured the view into a brick-walled backyard.

"You're late"' Mrs Maling said.

"I'm sorry," said Martin. "I was watching the rag-and-bone man. I haven't seen him for ages."

"It's about time he gave up, the old rascal," she replied. "He's been pushing that pram round the town for as long as I can remember. He must be over seventy by now." Despite her tone she obviously had a soft spot for the unsavoury gentleman.

She was a short stout person shaped rather like a little barrel and would be in her early fifties. Her grey hair was drawn back from her face into a large bun tied high on the back of her head and she had on a grey dress over which she wore a dark blue cardigan with an old-fashioned brooch fastened to the collar. Her face was rounded, the flesh hanging on either side of her mouth in dainty folds that quivered when she got excited or upset. She had been a widow for fifteen years.

Martin remarked that it looked as though it was going to be a wet day again and Mrs Maling agreed, adding that it had been sunny first thing when she cleaned the step but that the best part of the day where the weather was concerned now seemed to be over.

"I had a letter from Doris this morning," she continued, passing him a cup of tea. "She asked to be remembered to you."

Martin felt uneasy. There was something slightly unnatural about the way Mrs Maling was talking as if she had been rehearsing what she was going to say. He could only remember her having sounded like this once before and this had been when she had been working round to ask him for more money towards his keep. This was unlikely to be the problem today.

"That's nice of her," he answered, sounding equally unnatural. "How is she getting along?" Doris was Mrs Maling's daughter, a childhood companion of his, some years older than he was, who had married and was now living away from the district.

The Trip Back

"She wishes she was nearer here so that she could see me more often," said Mrs Maling. "She misses her old home. It's so far away where she is and so cut off."

Martin felt a touch of perspiration on his upper lip. He would have liked to jump up and say he must go, that he was late or something but he could hardly abandon the breakfast she had prepared for him. There was certainly trouble brewing. He could see her face quivering and she could not look into his eyes any more than he could look into hers. Had she noticed something different about him after all?

"Its must be a big change living in the country after being in the town," he said.

"Yes," she replied and here the conversation came to a stop for the time being.

Martin ate his breakfast as quickly as he could but when Mrs Maling poured more tea, felt he had to say something and said the first thing that came into his head. "Is there anything on the television tonight?"

"There's the football at half-past nine, Mrs Maling said. "That should be worth watching." Her husband had been keen on sport and she had maintained his interest, believing, as she put it, that this was what he would have wished. She watched all the televised football matches and expected Martin to do the same when he was at home. Hers was one of the first television sets in the street, bought mainly because of the sport.

"I shall look forward to seeing it," he replied.

Having now finished his breakfast, he got up from the table and had almost reached the door when Mrs Maling asked, "Will you be home for dinner today?" On other days he took sandwiches to eat at the shop but on Wednesdays, early closing day, he came home at lunchtime or had done so until two months ago.

"No," he said. "I'm sorry. I meant to tell you."

"Or for tea?"

"No."

There was a pause.

"That friend of yours is taking a long time to get better, isn't he? It's weeks since you've been home on a Wednesday."

Martin did not like the direction in which the conversation was going. "Yes, but he's all right now," he said. "I shan't have to see him again after this week."

"It's funny your not mentioning this friend till he got taken ill two months ago."

Martin groped for a lie. "He's someone who helped us at the shop during the summer holidays."

Mrs Maling pressed her hands together, her face quivering with a mixture of anger and distress. "Oh, Martin!" she said. "How can you tell me such a lot of lies? There's no friend, is there? Do you think I can't tell when you're lying? I've known for weeks you haven't been going to see a sick friend. I didn't say anything because I thought you were just making excuses to go out with some girl but it's not that, is it?"

She did not wait for him to answer. "No, of course it's not," she went on. "If it is, it's a very funny sort of girl! If you could see yourself when you come home on Wednesdays! Giggling - that's the only word for it! - giggling to yourself and when I ask you what's funny, you say, 'Nothing,' or that it's something comical you just thought of that happened at work. If it wasn't for your breath not smelling I'd think you'd been on the booze. Your face is as red as if you had been. But if its not the drink, what is it?"

She was looking straight into his face now, having previously addressed her words to the wallpaper above his head and he was disturbed to see that her eyes were glassy as if she were going to cry.

"It's nothing," he said, hoping to avoid an explanation either now or later. "Nothing to get upset about, I assure you. I can't tell you about it now or I shall be late for work. Look at the time! I must go or Mr Higlis will be giving me the sack!"

But Mrs Maling's eyes, formerly close to tears, had hardened. "No" she said. "We are going to have this out here and now! Mr Higlis can wait for once! I want to know what you get up to on Wednesdays and why you're so different then. Can't you see I'm worried about you - and afraid? Afraid of seeing you come home at night making that silly giggling noise with your face all red and most of all I'm afraid because of your eyes!"

"My eyes!" thought Martin. "She's noticed my eyes!"

"They're black," she said. "Not pale and grey like they are now but big and black like lumps of coal. How could anyone's eyes change colour? It doesn't make sense. The drink couldn't do that. I lie awake wondering what's happening and what I ought to do. When your parents had to move away and you came to live here I said I'd keep an eye on you on their behalf. I can't believe you're the sort of person to get into trouble but I don't understand what you've been up to lately and unless you tell me what it is I shall have no choice. I shall have to tell your parents."

Martin was dismayed at the thought of his parents being brought into this. It would be bad enough explaining to Mrs Maling, if he had to, and then it would only be half the story, but they would never understand. One thing was certain: he could not tell her anything until today was over. In the meantime all he could do was to try and stall her.

He returned to the table and sat facing her. "Mrs Maling, please don't tell them," he said. "I promise you I've done nothing to be ashamed of."

"Then why can't you tell me about it?"

"Because I don't think you would understand. It's a personal thing. In any case, it's true what I said about today being the last time. There's no point in upsetting my parents over something that'll be over and done with before they even get your letter. Can't you see that?"

Mrs Maling's eyes started to moisten. From her cardigan pocket she pulled out a small handkerchief and proceeded to dab at the tears though it looked inadequate to cope with the flow. She was not one to miss the opportunity for an indulgence of emotion. After blowing her nose, she paused and then went on, more to herself than to Martin, "We'll talk about it tonight when you come home. If it really is the last time there'll be no point in writing. The last thing I want to do is to worry your parents unnecessarily."

She stared at him. "Will you be coming home like that again tonight?"

"No," Martin said, crossing his fingers under the table and hoping he was telling the truth. "Definitely not!" He then got to his feet, pushing the chair away from him. "I must go now," he told her. "Don't worry about it any more."

Before she could delay him further he escaped into the hall where a pair of stuffed animal heads hung on either side of a bulky barometer. He tried to erase the picture from his mind of Mrs Maling sitting there in the next room in a tearful state because of him. He felt guilty at having been the cause of her distress but to have told her the full story would only have upset her more. He wiped his hand across his forehead. This was going to be a bad day - he could see that - the worst Wednesday of the lot! First, that awful feeling when he woke up, now a scene with Mrs Maling, and soon a row with Mr Higlis about being late for work. Even the barometer, whose pointer was fast returning to "Rain", was against him!

Grabbing his mackintosh, he let himself out through the front door, avoiding the step that Mrs Maling had been diligently cleaning while he was getting dressed. As he stepped outside under a now gloomy sky, he shouted "Goodbye," and was glad to hear her reply in her usual voice as he shut the door.

It was fifteen minutes' walk to work following almost the same route as the children took to go to school. From Mrs Maling's to the bottom of the street was about two hundred yards, then you turned into Norton Avenue, where the houses were bigger and had front gardens with lawns and shrubs. There were also trees growing on the pavement on either side of the street though their leaves had fallen at this time of the year and long vanished down gutters and drains. The residents of Norton Avenue considered themselves a cut above the people in Martin's street, where there was no greenery, and walkers going to or from the town tended to cross automatically to the other side of the road where there were no houses, just a tall continuous brick wall with broken glass on top to discourage climbers from getting into the private grounds beyond. The wall was less interesting to walk beside but it always seemed pleasanter on that side of the road than on the other with its houses and air of aloofness.

Norton Avenue led eventually to the main street or what was the beginning of the main street, for it was still a good half-mile to the centre of the town. The shops at this end were small and looked as though they could do with a coat of paint but business was not

The Trip Back

good in this part of the town and the proprietors had little money to spare for improvements.

At the corner of Norton Avenue with the main street stood a cinema called the "Royal", the name of which was spelt out in neon lighting on the wall above the pseudo-marble portico. When lit up at night the lettering was a quivering red and could be seen from a long way off beckoning customers.

When Martin used to go to school, he reckoned he could run as far as the "Royal" without stopping but by then he usually had the stitch and had to walk slowly until it had worn off. He now tried running the same distance but had to give up in Norton Avenue because he was out of practice and out of breath. He ran and walked alternately following the tall brick wall on the opposite side of the road from the houses till reaching the busier main street.

It was the first time he had been in a real hurry since his schooldays and he was surprised how his eyes kept picking out little landmarks which he had forgotten but which were now coming back to him as he found himself hurrying that way again, counting every minute as he had done as a boy. There was a single yellow brick among all the red ones in that high wall; a tree with a mouth-like hole in it, where the bark was deformed, and a stain of blue on the pavement where someone had once upset a tin of paint. All these had been milestones for measuring his progress when he was a child racing to school after playing too long or dawdling over his meal.

At the "Royal" Martin plucked up courage to look at his wristwatch and saw it was quarter-past nine, no less than fifteen minutes after the shop had opened! He started running again, weaving in and out of the pedestrians who were more numerous than they had been in the side streets and at length he reached the river bridge over half his journey behind him. It was a stone bridge consisting of two spans across the stream, flowing slowly and muddily below. There was a willow tree here and there but mostly it was untidy yards and sheds occupying the river's edge. As he crossed the bridge the sun, which had been hidden behind clouds, came out for a moment and the brown water dazzled as it reflected the unexpected light. From the centre of the bridge he could see the church tower with its gilded clock face and was cheered to notice that its hands gave the time as five minutes earlier than his wristwatch though he realised the church clock had a reputation for being slow.

On the other side of the bridge the road began to rise and the shops became larger and more prosperous looking as the centre of the town drew nearer. A grocer's shop stood on the corner of School Road, which went off to the right, and nailed to the wall above it was a large metal plate bearing an advertising sign of a stag leaping a chasm to escape from the hunters. On his way to and from school, on those occasions when there had been no need to hurry, Martin had lingered beneath this picture, building all kinds of fantasies around it. He had imagined himself astride the stag's back being carried safely from one cliff edge to the other or jumping the chasm unaided, like the stag, leaving behind his pursuers, too afraid to jump the gap after him. The picture was not as vividly coloured now as it had been in those days and there were rust marks coming through the plate in places but it still looked bold and romantic up there above the street, that gallant stag leaping against a brilliant blue sky.

In his school days Martin would have turned off beneath the picture because School Road, as its name implied, led eventually to the school, but to get to work he had to continue up the main streets towards the town centre. There were wet areas in front of the shops where the lowlier members of staff had been mopping down the paved entrances to their premises, a job Martin would have been doing if he had been on time. A fair-haired young man in a grey suit was still outside one of the shops with a mop and bucket and looked surprised when he saw Martin approaching. "What's happened to you this morning?" he said. "You're a bit late, aren't you?"

Martin, who was too out of breath to reply, gestured as if to say it was not his fault and ran past the youth who laughed unsympathetically. "I wouldn't like to be you when Higlis sees you'" he called. There was another young man on the opposite pavement and he looked across the street and grinned too.

It was twenty-past-nine by his watch when Martin arrived at the glass and chrome front of Mackie's shoe shop where he was employed. He noticed that someone had already washed down the entrance and knew that it must have been Miss Cutts. Trust Higlis to humiliate him by making her do it! As he went inside she was talking to the manager at the far end of the shop but they stopped and turned as they saw him push open the glass door.

Mr Higlis came down the shop, puffing himself out to look formidable but succeeding only in looking absurd. He was a short man with thin grey hair brushed tightly against his scalp, and a little gingery moustache that he kept immaculately cut.

Dressed as usual in a dark suit, white shirt, grey tie and shiny black shoes, he had an over-polished, almost puppet-like appearance. With his eyes glittering behind metal-framed glasses, he said to Martin as fiercely as he could, "What's the meaning of this? I suppose you realise it's half-past nine?"

Martin felt in no position to argue the accuracy of the time. "I'm sorry," he said, but a simple apology was by no means enough for the manager.

"You know I insist on punctuality," he said. "How can I run a business otherwise" He paused significantly. "Being late is not going to improve your prospects with the firm, is it? How can I recommend you for a transfer if you're unpunctual?" This question had a sting in it because Martin wanted a transfer to Mackie's branch in the town where his parents were living and needed Mr Higlis's co-operation to get it, as the dapper shop manager knew only too well.

"I had some trouble at my digs" Martin said, having abandoned his original idea of saying that he had stopped to give help at the scene of an accident. This could be investigated and found to be false besides, he doubted whether Mr Higlis would have believed him anyway.

"What happens at your lodgings is no concern of mine," the shop manager replied.' Your private life should not be allowed to get in the way of your work." He paused again. "You realise, of course, that Miss Cutts has had to wash down the front"

Again the question had a sting in it. Mr Higlis knew that Martin and Miss Cutts were friends and that Martin would resent her having to do this task because of him. "I thought you might have left it till I arrived," he said.

"Oh"' exclaimed Mr Higlis. "And how was I to know when that was going to be? No, Martin, If you fail to turn up on time, someone else must do your work for you." His tone then modified as if a different, more generous role were now called for. "Fortunately, this morning's lapse is more the exception than the rule as far as you're concerned and I am prepared to overlook it provided the same thing does not happen again."

He again puffed himself out, this time trying to look magnanimous but again only looking absurd.

"Thank you, Mr Higlis," said Martin, trying to look as grateful as he could.

"Very well," said the manager. "And now I suggest you make up for lost time by getting the sun blinds down."

Martin stared. "But it's going to rain," he said.

"We shall meet that eventuality if and when it arises," Mr Higlis said and walked off.

After Martin had pulled down the blinds he re-entered the showroom and walked through to the back office and storeroom where a newly-arrived consignment of rubber boots was waiting to be unpacked. Through a glass panel in the door he could see several customers coming into the shop but Mr Higlis and Miss Cutts appeared well able to cope with them and he felt it wiser to stay out of the way for a while. He had not yet had a chance to talk to Miss Cutts but as he went through the showroom she had given him a smile, which made him feel better.

As he was entering the rubber boots in the stock register, she looked round the door and said, "He's gone to the bank. Come and keep me company out here." Martin went into the showroom and the two of them stood leaning against the shelves of white boxes, keeping an eye on the door for any customer who might come in, the shop being empty for the time being.

"I'm terribly sorry about your having to wash down the front this morning," Martin said.

Miss Cutts laughed. "That's all right," she said. "It brought back memories of my long-lost youth. I haven't done that job for years. I almost asked him whether I could borrow a pair of waders from stock to stop my feet from getting splashed but luckily I had a pair of old shoes here. Mind you, I wouldn't want to have to do it too often! Anyway, what happened to you this morning?"

"I had a row with my landlady," Martin said.

"I can't imagine you having a row with anyone" she replied. "Just look at the way you let old Higlis trample all over you this morning. If I'd been you I'd soon have put him in his place! You've been here for nearly three years and haven't been late once to my certain knowledge. Why didn't you tell him that? If he can't put up with your coming late just once in three years, he's even more obnoxious than I thought he was'"

I can't afford to rub him up the wrong way," said Martin. "I'm depending on him to fix my transfer to the branch where my parents are should the opportunity arise. I wouldn't put it past him to refuse if he felt like turning nasty."

"Would that be such a bad thing - if you didn't get your transfer?"

Martin looked at her with surprise. He was about to ask what she meant when a woman customer came in with a small child and Miss Cutts went to attend to them.

Martin gazed after her. She was considerably older than he was, probably getting on for fifty, but he was not conscious of the difference in their ages. She was someone whose company he enjoyed, who could be depended on to be lively and cheerful no matter how trying the day might be at the shop. Her full-lipped mouth, lightly touched with lipstick, always seemed to be smiling or on the verge of smiling. She was a good-looking woman and he sometimes wondered why she had never married. She was very independent, as Mr Higlis often found out when he tried arguing with her, and it was perhaps because she had not wished to forgo her independence that she had chosen to stay single. Martin was sure she could have got married if she had wanted to. Her figure was getting plump now but she dressed carefully and her wavy brown hair, threaded with grey, was stylishly done. She wore a black dress to work and though it was quite plain, apart from a marcasite brooch at the neckline, it looked elegant on her.

After she had dealt with the customer she returned to Martin who, referring to their interrupted conversation, said, "What did you mean by saying, 'Would it be a bad thing if I didn't get my transfer?"

"Forget it, Martin," she said. "I was interfering as usual."

"No, I would like to hear," he said. "You must have had a reason."

"All right," she said, "but you won't like it. What I meant was that having made the break with your parents, why go back to them? You've got to admit that when they lived here they kept you tied tightly to their apron strings. And when they left, they appointed that landlady of yours as a watchdog to keep an eye on you. I bet you're almost as much under her thumb as you were under theirs."

Miss Cutts's hand went up to her neck and began fingering the brooch on her dress. "I'm sorry if I've offended you, Martin," she said. "I shouldn't have said it but I want to see you making the most of life, not running away from it."

Maybe I've got something to run away from," he said.

"That's silly," she replied. "There's nothing wrong with you. What good is going back to your parents going to do?"

"I know they fuss over me," said Martin, "but I feel... well, safe with them." He regretted the word the minute he had said it. Indeed he did not know why he had said it. He would certainly not have done so two months ago.

"Safe!" Miss Cutts exclaimed. "What do you want to be safe for?" She laughed. "At your age you ought to be living dangerously well, not dangerously but you know what I mean' Now what are you smiling at?"

Martin said, "A few moments ago you were accusing my parents of telling me what to do and now you are doing the same thing!"

"I suppose I am," she replied, "but it's because we're friends and I want to see you opening up instead of closing in on yourself." She turned to him, pulling a face to express indignation. "And that's another thing, Martin! You're so secretive! Each Wednesday for the past two months you've been racing off at one o'clock to catch a bus and not a word to anyone about where you're going or what you're doing. I suppose that later on this morning you'll be putting in another request for me to cover up while you slip off early."

Martin was put out by her question. He had been wondering how to broach the subject and now that it had been thrown right at him he did not know quite what to say. Miss Cutts had no more idea than Mrs Maling about what he did on Wednesdays but would not press him for an explanation as his landlady had done. In fairness to Mrs Maling, however, Miss Cutts had never seen him directly after one of his "transformations." "Well, as a matter of fact, I was hoping that you could help me out again this week," he said.

"I thought as much," she replied. "For two pins I wouldn't do it unless you let me in on your secret. How many weeks is it you owe me now?"

"This will be the last Wednesday, "Martin said, "and then I can start paying you back. If I can get away as soon as Mr Higlis goes, it gives me a chance to catch the five-past-one bus. There isn't another for half-an-hour and that's too late. I don't like leaving you to do the cash and lock up but I'll do it myself from next week for as long as you like and you can get away early every Wednesday if you want to."

"What would an old maid like me want with getting away early on her afternoon off?" replied Miss Cutts with a smile. "There was a time when I used to count the minutes to early closing but not any more, Martin. I don't mind finishing off here if you want to get away. I shan't even insist on your explaining what you get up to though I don't mind telling you I'd love to know."

Before Martin could thank her - or evade the hint that he should confide in her - the glass door swung open at the front of the shop and Mr Higlis came in, stamping his wet shoes on the mat and folding a sodden umbrella. "It's raining," he said. "Those sun blinds will have to go up again, Martin, They ought never to have come down in the first place."

Martin glanced at Miss Cutts whose eyes twinkled in reply. "Yes, Mr Higlis," he said. "Right away."

It was true about the rain. It was pouring down and the sky looked full of it. He would be having a wet journey that afternoon. Martin put his raincoat over his head while he grappled with the blinds and afterwards stood in the porch shaking the coat dry before re-entering the showroom. He was followed in by Colonel Wellum, who was on the town council and presided at the local magistrates' court. On seeing his customer, Mr Higlis stepped forward, glowing. "How nice to see you, Colonel," he said. "It must be over a year since you were last here."

The Colonel muttered that it was and that he wanted to get fixed up with a pair of boots before the winter set in. For a few minutes the two men stood talking about the weather and affairs of the town, then the manager asked Colonel Wellum what sort of boots he would like to try on. The Colonel, an upright, bulky man with a brusque way of talking, looked round till he saw Martin. "If you don't mind, Higlis, "he said. I'll let that young fellow of yours attend to me. He knows by now what my requirements are."

Mr Higlis was annoyed. "I have no doubt I could attend to you satisfactorily myself," he said.

"Nor have I, old chap," the Colonel replied, "but I know what a busy fellow you are and I wouldn't want to waste your time unnecessarily." Mr Higlis was about to interrupt but the Colonel went on, "So ask the laddie to come over, will you? Let's wear the young ones out first."

The shop manager, who was very angry, turned and went over to Martin. "Attend to Colonel Wellum!" he said sharply. "He seems to think you know more about this business than I do!' From the way in which Colonel Wellum had been glancing at him, Martin had sensed what was going on and the effect it would have on Mr Higlis. To be asked for by an important customer was gratifying but hardly worth the reprisals that would undoubtedly follow from a jealous Mr Higlis.

"I hope I haven't queered your pitch with the manager," Colonel Wellum whispered as Martin joined him, "but I can't stand that silly little man fussing over me. Besides, he always tries to make me have what I don't want. Now you're a sensible lad. You don't waste time arguing about whether I'm old-fashioned or not. You just give me the footwear I want."

"Yes, sir," said Martin. "But you're right about Mr Higlis. He's not going to like it at all. Nines, broad fitting, isn't it? I think we've got the same in stock that you had last time if you'd care to try them on."

The Trip Back

Mr Higlis went upstairs.

After a satisfied Colonel Wellum had left the shop, Martin joined Miss Cutts, who was typing letters in the office. "You saw what happened?" he asked. "Yes," she said. "I'm afraid you're in for it, Martin! I wonder how and when the blow will fall?"

"Well, it's raining hard," said Martin. "I expect he will shortly ask me to deliver a special parcel to the farthest end of the town on foot and preferably without a mackintosh!"

Miss Cutts laughed. "Perhaps he'll leave it till tomorrow," she said. It's half-past eleven already. He's only got another hour-and-a-half to think something up."

But Mr Higlis was wasting no time and when the blow fell it was still only ten minutes to twelve. Miss Cutts had gone out to the post office and Martin was serving an elderly woman who seemed more interested in enjoying a sit-down and keeping out of the rain than in making a purchase. Mr Higlis, who had been moving about upstairs, re-appeared down the staircase and crossed to where Martin was kneeling beside his customer.

"Have you any idea where the cricket boots are?" he said. "I've looked for them everywhere."

"They're up in the attic," Martin replied. "We put them there in September at the end of the season."

"Of course," said Mr Higlis. "I remember now. Would you mind looking out a pair for me? I'll attend to this lady while you're gone."

Martin put down the shoebox he was holding, feeling a stab of dismay as he realised what the shop manager was up to. "But the cricket season is over," he said. "That's why we put the boots away."

"I know," said Mr Higlis, "but I had a man inquiring about cricket boots yesterday. Apparently he's going abroad and wants to take a pair with him."

"But can't it wait until later?" Martin said with an edge to his voice.

"No," said Mr Higlis. "He said he would call back again either today or tomorrow and I want to be ready for him, so get along, there's a good lad! We don't want to keep this lady waiting."

His eyes, framed by their metal-rimmed glasses, gleamed as he observed Martin's discomfiture. "Well, what are you waiting for?" he said. "It's size eight we want."

The woman customer looked up at the two men with interest, unaware of what was going on but sensing the tension between them. Martin gave in when he saw her watching, knowing that he could not afford to have a scene in front of a customer. He knew that Mr Higlis's story about the cricket boots was a lie and that it was just an excuse to get him to go up to the attic in the hope that he would make a fool of himself as he had done on other occasions when alone up there.

Putting down the shoebox, he got to his feet and walked slowly over to the foot of the carpeted staircase, where he began ascending the stairs, feeling Mr Higlis's eyes on him all the way till he had disappeared into the first floor.

Mackie's was a tall, narrow building squeezed between other shops and was far longer than it was wide. It had two upper storeys - three if one included the roof attic - neither of which was more than the width of an average room across though both extended a long way back. The first floor ran the full length of the building with a large sash window at either end letting in plenty of light, and it was here that overflow stock was kept. Sometimes customers were allowed up if it was more convenient to serve them on this floor.

Against the back wall was a staircase rising to the next floor, not as wide as the stairs from the ground floor and covered with worn linoleum instead of a carpet. Martin went up these stairs till he reached the second floor, which had only one small window, where the top of the staircase was, and was poorly lit.

This floor was long and narrow, too, but was not open like the floor below. It was divided into several small compartments opening off a corridor which got gradually darker as it left the window behind. These compartments were little more than cubbyholes used for storing window display stands and showroom equipment though one contained an old tap and sink, unused now because a proper washroom had since been provided on the ground floor at the back of the shop.

Martin rested a moment at the top of the stairs, looking along this quiet corridor, which began in the light of the window and led through twilight to the dark corner at the far end. It was this corner and the darkness cloaking it that disturbed Martin. Usually when he came up to the attic he was accompanied by Mr Higlis or Miss Cutts because it was easier to pass down goods from the attic above if there was someone waiting to take them at the foot of the steep, ladder-like steps which had to be mounted.

Occasionally he had come up on his own and something had happened: something that he had at first tried to pass off as an unexpected "bad turn" though when it had happened a second time this explanation sounded less plausible and on the third and last occasion it was apparent that his behaviour, far from being coincidental, was actually caused in some way by his presence alone on that upper floor.

Martin had to admit that he sometimes experienced what he could best describe as an uneasy feeling when confronted by a sudden dark corner though the feeling could be easily overcome either by waiting a moment or two or, where possible, by going another way. With the attic stairs, however, it was different because he knew he had to climb them because Mr Higlis had told him to. If he had been able to choose it would not have been so bad. Why he should get this feeling was something that he did not understand. He could think of no reason for it.

Before attempting to walk along the corridor Martin paused to look out of the small dirty back window at the plateau of untidy roofs and chimneys beyond, all streaming with rain. The gush of the rain was all that he could hear apart from his wristwatch ticking loudly in the silence. Though it was rainy and dull the window still let in a fair amount of light and when he reached the far end of the corridor he would still not be more than a dozen paces from it if he wanted to turn back. But he was not going to turn back. This was what Mr Higlis wanted him to do: to make a fool of himself as he had done on those other occasions. He was going to forget what happened before. This time everything was going to be all right. He was going to walk quietly along the corridor, turn the corner at the far end, switch on the light and go up the attic stairs after which there would he nothing to worry about.

"You can't do it! You haven't got the nerve!" That was the voice in his brain cutting in again after leaving him alone for a couple of hours! Trust it to re-emerge just when he least wanted to hear from it! Martin ignored the voice - or tried to! - and looking at his wristwatch saw that it was seven minutes to twelve. By the time it was twelve o'clock he would be back downstairs in the showroom again, Mr Higlis would have his cricket boots - and much good might they do him! - and this episode would be nothing more than a joke to share with Miss Cutts.

Slowly Martin began walking along the corridor: the light of the window receded and the shadows came out to meet him. He touched the door handles of the cubicles, then reached a point only two or three feet from the corner. He would see where the right-hand wall of the corridor ended, a vertical slash of white with the darkness beyond.

Martin knew what was round the corner. There was an electric switch where he would turn on the light; there were the attic stairs, steep, open and wooden and more like a ladder really, and there, through an opening in the ceiling, was the attic itself, where they stored out-of-season footwear or specialist stock for which there was little regular demand. All that he had to do was to turn the corner, put his hand on the light switch and ascend the stairs. Why, therefore, had he stopped walking?

Martin was fascinated by that vertical white edge of the corner, dividing the wall from the darkness, the seen from the unseen. All that he had to do was to step beyond that line. Why then, was he not moving?

He rested himself against the wall unable at least for the moment to go further. He was also anxious, subconsciously at first, not to make a noise, almost as if he felt he was no longer alone, and when he began to think openly about why he was keeping so quiet, it was then that he realised that this was exactly what he did believe: that there was something waiting there on the other side, just as it had done on those previous occasions.

Cautiously he flattened himself against the wall, his back and arms pressed against it, and stood there listening, just a couple of feet from the corner where the unseen began. If, as he believed, there was something waiting for him, it was obviously trying not to give itself away yet Martin knew it was there, could almost hear it breathing, and he simply dared not move. All that he could do was

The Trip Back

to go on waiting, hoping that whatever it was would eventually go away; and as he stood there silently, rigidly, he could hear the traffic in the street not far away and the rain pattering on the window at the other end of the corridor, ordinary sounds which should have been comforting but which made the silence seem all the greater. Perspiration began to appear on his forehead and he had to close his eyelids to stop it from seeping into and stinging his eyes.

And with his eyes shut he could now build up a picture in his mind of what sort of thing it was waiting for him, the creature growing larger and larger, like a genie emerging from a bottle, till its presences engulfed Martin, wrapping him in a suffocating cloud, and he could neither stand still nor keep quiet a moment longer. His heart was beating so loudly that the corridor seemed to echo with the noise and as tears pushed open his eyes he uttered a sound that he knew must be the end of him. The walls, ceiling and floor began rotating and he could feel himself falling. The floor came up to meet him and he threw up his hands to stop his face from crashing against the boards.

The thump of Martin hitting the floor resonated through the building to the ground floor of the shop. Mr Higlis looked up and so did Miss Cutts, who had just come back from the post office, her hair wet from the rain. There were two women customers in the shop who raised their faces towards the ceiling where the electric light bowls were swaying slightly.

"What was that, Mr Higlis?" asked one of the women.

Miss Cutts looked at the shop manager, her face angry as she realised what had happened. "You didn't send him up to the attic, did you?" she said.

"I did ask him to do a little task for me up there, yes," Mr Higlis replied smugly.

"How could you!" Miss Cutts exclaimed, "knowing this might happen!" and pulling off her raincoat she hurried across the showroom and up the carpeted stairs, ignoring the two women staring after her.

When she had gone Mr Higlis turned to the customers and winked. He was in a rare good humour. "What it is to have temperamental staff!" he said, and laughed.

On reaching the top floor, Miss Cutts could see Martin lying at the end of the corridor and after filling a cup from the washroom tap, knelt beside him, holding the water to his lips. When he had drunk and was obviously recovering, she said, "What happened, Martin? Was it the same as last time?"

"Yes," Martin replied. "I've made a fool of myself again. That was what Mr Higlis wanted me to do, of course. He sent me up here deliberately hoping this would happen. I can't think what makes it happen. I kept telling myself as I came up the stairs that I would be all right this time."

He lifted himself up into a sitting position and leaned his head against the wall. "I think it must be because I know I've got to go round this corner to do what Mr Higlis says. If it happens in other places I don't have to go on. I can wait or go some other way and this makes it easier."

Martin smiled. "It's stupid, isn't it?"

"Does it happen often?" Miss Cutts asked.

"No, not really, I can't say when it's going to happen. It just comes out of the blue. I suddenly find myself shaking before that edge you know, that vertical edge where the corner is, and I can't get round it, and I begin to think silly things - well, about something unpleasant waiting for me. It's so stupid! I feel ashamed just talking about it."

Miss Cutts paused. "What happens to you may not be so stupid," she said. "It could be you've got some sort of phobia like people have about being shut in or on high places. If you were to see a doctor, I'm sure he could help you. I think you ought to see a doctor, Martin. As long as you have this whatever it is you are never going to be really sure of yourself, are you? For one thing, you will always be at the mercy of that little sadist downstairs!"

Her voice was so friendly, her presence so reassuring that Martin, still feeling shaken, impulsively decided to tell her everything about Wednesdays. If anyone was likely to understand, she would. If it spoilt their friendship, if she could no longer respect him, this was a risk he would have to take. The way he felt at this moment, he just could not get through another Wednesday on his own.

"Miss Cutts," he said, feeling relieved to be confiding in someone at last, "I did see a doctor like you said about two months ago..."

There were footsteps on the stairs and a dapper figure appeared in outline against the grubby window at the end of the corridor. It was Mr Higlis.

"I don't know what's going on up here," he said, "but I'm entirely on my own in the shop. I try to allow my staff a certain amount of latitude but I do not intend to be exploited. One of you will have to come down immediately."

He gazed at the two figures and though Martin could not see his eyes he could picture them gloating. "Did you have a fall a moment or two ago, Martin?" he asked. "I hope you didn't hurt yourself. Falling down up here seems to be getting quite a habit with you, doesn't it? Next time one of us will have to come up with you and hold your hand!" He laughed, then snapped, "Well, one of you had better come down at once. You know how busy we are during the last hour before closing!"

As he turned to descend the stairs, Martin called after him, "What about the cricket boots, Mr Higlis? Do you still want them?"

"Oh, no, "the voice came back, "You'd better leave them to me. I've come to the conclusion that if you want anything done in this shop it's best to do it yourself!"

"That man's a menace!" Miss Cutts hissed, rising to her feet and pushing into place a lock of hair that had fallen over her forehead. It was not often one saw her with her hair out of place.

"He ought to be locked up in clink," she went on, "or better still put away in Holtwood with all the other loonies." She started walking along the corridor towards the top of the stairs. "I suppose I'd better do as he says. What were you telling me, Martin, before he came, about seeing a doctor? Did it do any good?"

But Martin had recovered himself now. No, she would not understand if he told her. He could see that now. He was glad Mr Higlis had arrived when he did to prevent him from giving himself away. "I suppose so," he lied. "He told me it was nothing to worry about. In time I would grow out of it, he said."

"There may be some truth in that," Miss Cutts replied, believing him. "It's surprising how you change as you get older. At one time, before mother died, I thought I wouldn't be able to spend the night in the house on my own but look at me now! I have to do it all the time. I'm glad you saw a doctor, though, Martin. It's a good thing to know you don't have to worry."

She heard him following her along the corridor. "Are you coming down, too?" she said.

"Yes, I'm all right now," he replied, "and sorry for the trouble I've caused. Let's hope it won't happen again." He was remembering that this unpleasant episode had changed nothing. It was just another incident in a day that had started badly and showed no signs of improving as it went along. It was always the same when he wanted to be sure of himself: things kept happening to undermine his confidence. The most difficult and important part of the day still lay ahead: he still had to confront them and tell them straight that he was having nothing more to do with them and this was going to take all the confidence he could muster. But at least the morning was over. In the distance he could hear the church clock striking noon.

2. AFTERNOON

Mr Higlis left early as Martin expected. At five-to-one he put on his hat, coat and silk scarf and said, "I'll leave it to the two of you to check the cash and lock up. Mrs Higlis is not very well again and I want to get back as soon as I can." This was his usual reason for leaving early though on those occasions when his wife called at the shop she looked the picture of health. "In the morning," he added, "we must have a go at the shop window. It must be over three weeks since we put in that display. Good day to you both! Have a pleasant afternoon!"

After giving him time to get clear of the shop, Martin glanced at Miss Cutts. "Is it all right for me to go then?" he asked.

"Yes," she said. "I can look after things here," adding mischievously, "unless you like to hang on a minute or two and take me with you." Though he knew she was only joking Martin could not help feeling embarrassed. "Oh, I don't think you'd like it where I'm going," he said quickly, then wondered whether he ought to have said this - whether it might somehow have given him away.

"I'll take your word for it, Martin," she laughed. "Not that I'd want to go off on a jaunt on a rotten afternoon like this. Well, run along them: I'll see you tomorrow."

"Tomorrow'" thought Martin as he collected his raincoat and slipped out of the shop. How wonderful the word sounded! By tomorrow there would be no more secrets to be kept, no more lies to be told and hopefully he could put the past two months behind him and forget they had ever happened. By tomorrow he would be rid of those people who had led him into this nightmare, there would be no more need to go dashing off early to catch buses and Wednesday could return to being an ordinary day like any other.

The bus station was in a large square at the back of the Town Hall, only a couple of minutes' walk away. The rain was not falling as fast now and he carried his raincoat over his arm as he hurried through the crowds emptying from the shops, where doors were being closed and lights switched off for early closing. Then he reached the bus station it was nearly five-past-one, the time when his bus was due to leave, and a "170" was standing at the rank with the driver already in his seat and the conductress standing on the rear platform with her arm raised to pull the bell cord. Martin caught hold of the upright column to jump aboard but stopped as he raised his foot on the platform, aware for the first time of the mistake he was making.

What a fool he was! Why was he hurrying like this? If he meant to get his own way, if he really wanted this to be the last Wednesday, he ought not to be racing to catch the bus, just as he had done during previous weeks. They had often told him how essential it was for him to be there on time, that it was a waste of time his coming otherwise. If he arrived late there would be no question of his being persuaded to do anything he did not want to for the simple reason that the time would not allow it. The argument would have been settled before he even arrived. If they were angry and wanted to know why he was late, he could make up an excuse - say that he had been kept at the shop or missed the bus, which would be so much easier than arriving at the proper time and having to argue with them and risk being defeated.

"Well, make up your mind, love!" he heard the bus conductress say. "Are you coming or aren't you?"

Withdrawing his hand from the column, Martin stepped back on the pavement, looking up at her blankly. "Please yourself," she said with a shrug. "There isn't another for half-an-hour!"

Still struggling to decide whether to go or not, Martin went on standing there immobile until his mind was made up for him. "Hold tight, please!" he heard the conductress shout as she jerked the bell cord, and he felt a blast of air in his face as the bus moved off without him.

It was one of the few times in his life that he had deliberately disobeyed anyone. He had been told to be there as near half-past one as possible and now the earliest he could arrive was after two. He could hardly believe what he had done! With half-and-hour to go before the next bus he could see no point in hanging about, agonising about whether he had acted wisely or not, and decided the best thing was to occupy the time by having something to eat and he therefore made his way towards the small glass-roofed refreshment room on an island in the centre of the bus park. As he walked across the tarmac the rain began to fall heavily again and he had to run the last few yards to prevent himself from getting wet.

It was hot and noisy in the refreshment room, crowded with shoppers waiting for the buses home. There was also a sprinkling of dark uniformed bus drivers and conductors taking a break between journeys. At the counter Martin asked the woman for egg and chips and after paying was told to sit at a table till his order was called out. "I'll give you a shout when it's ready," she said. He found himself a place at a plastic-topped table where two middle-aged women were talking over cups of tea with their shopping stacked on the floor beside them.

Already he was regretting not having boarded the bus and if it had still been there he would have jumped up unhesitatingly and chased after it without waiting for his order. He had been foolish to risk annoying them, he could see that now. It occurred to him that as he had missed the bus it might be better not to go at all and to write explaining that he was not coming again but he was pretty sure they would not let him off this easily. They might try to get in touch with him at the shop or at his digs, which was the last thing he wanted.

"One egg and chips!" The woman's shrill voice cut across the hubbub and Martin went over to collect his order to which he asked her to add a cup of tea. Back at the table he tried eating but his inside was unreceptive. His stomach was throbbing as it had done when he woke that morning and his legs were feeling shaky again. The noise and the heat did not improve matters but it was no use going outside as long as the rain continued to beat down on the glass roof as it was at that moment.

Eventually he gave up trying to eat and pushed the plate away. The two women had gone and their place had been taken by an unshaven workman whose wet overalls smelled unpleasantly as they dried out in the heat of the room. People kept coming and going through the swing door, whose thumping to and fro added to the din. Among the newcomers was a tall, silver-haired bus conductor with thick black eyebrows and a taut, aggressive face.

Martin became aware of him because he sensed the man staring in his direction. He was leaning against the counter with a cup of tea in his hand and did not take his eyes off Martin for a moment, not even when raising the cup to his lips. Martin looked behind to see whether there was someone else who might be attracting the man's attention but no-one other than himself was directly in the path of that severe gaze. As he had not seen the man before as far as he knew, Martin assumed he could have no particular reason for looking at him but on returning the stare, he saw with alarm that the man's face was regarding him with unconcealed malevolence. He looked like someone who had unexpectedly come upon an enemy and was now about to settle old scores. Why a complete stranger should be looking at him like that Martin could not imagine! In an attempt to escape the stare he turned himself round but could still feel the eyes burning the back of his neck. The babble of voices was as deafening as ever and drops of condensation began to fall on his head from the glass roof, caused by the ascending steam of hot breath, damp clothes and too many over-heated bodies crammed into a small space.

Abandoning his half-full cup of tea, Martin jumped up, pulled on his raincoat and made for the swing door. Rain or no rain he was getting away from the noise, the heat and that man's stare! Out of the corner of his eye he could see the bus conductor put down his cup and step forward as if to follow him but the room was too crowded for him to move quickly and he dropped back to his position against the counter, keeping his eye on Martin all the way to the door.

Outside, Martin turned up his raincoat collar and stood under the eaves, prepared to wait there for ten minutes or so until the next bus was due to leave, but was glad to see a "170" already drawn up at the rank. He ran over to it and climbed the stairs to the upper deck, where he sat down and impatiently waited for the bus to leave. At that time he was the only person on board.

He was still the only passenger upstairs ten minutes later when he heard the engine start up and the bell cord ring for the driver to move off. As the bus turned out of the square he looked at his watch for the dozenth time since he got on board and saw they were leaving punctually, which meant there was a good chance he would get there soon after two. Seeing his face reflected in the window against a moving background of buildings, he felt suddenly disgusted with himself and could have thumped back at the reflection with his fist. What a coward he was! Half-an-hour ago he had deliberately missed the bus but now he was so scared of what he had done that he could not get to his destination quick enough. At least he could have stood by his decision and been properly late instead of dashing off on the next bus and fretting over every minute of the journey like some naughty child afraid of being punished. Angrily he turned his head away from the window, unable to bear the sight of the traitor staring back at him from the glass.

Other passengers were talking on the lower deck and he could hear the click of their tickets being punched by the conductor as he made his way along the bus. Soon there was the rasp of metal studded boots on the stairs as the conductor came up to see whether there was anyone on the upper deck. Martin held out his hand with a coin on it but drew it back when he saw that the conductor was the same man who had been scowling at him in the refreshment room. The conductor seemed equally surprised and leaned for a moment against the back of the seat, his black eyebrows closing together as he studied Martin's face. The floor tilted slightly and there was a swirl of buildings outside the window as the bus went round a corner sharply.

"Wood Corner, please," Martin said, holding out his money again, The black eyebrows separated and beneath them the eyes lit up spitefully. "I knew it was you!" the conductor exclaimed.

"That was where you got on last Wednesday, wasn't it?"

"Yes, why? What's the matter?" asked Martin, disturbed by the look on the man's face.

"You come on this bus - a '170' - from Wood Corner last Wednesday night, didn't you? At eight or thereabouts, after it was dark?"

"I don't know. Yes, I think so."

"I knew it was you. But you're not laughing at me now like you was then, are you? Tell me what was so funny last Wednesday night to make you want to laugh so much? Was it my face or my voice or what was it about me that you found so comical? Tell me!"

"I don't understand," said Martin.

"You got on this bus last Wednesday night and sat there giggling like some bloody schoolkid," the man said. "Each time I walked past you was sniggering behind your hand. You thought I didn't see you but I did! I would have had it out with you then but we was busy and I had other passengers to attend to and when I was ready you was gone, but I knew I would come across you again. I thought it was you when I saw you in the canteen but I wasn't sure because your face looks different from what it did last Wednesday. What have you done to your face? Or is it just because you're not laughing at me now?"

"If I was laughing," Martin replied, "I wasn't laughing at you?"

"No, then who was you laughing at? You know it was me. You started off the minute I handed you the ticket and kept on each time I looked at you. And don't try to make out you'd been drinking! I've been on nights long enough to know when a man's had a drink too many. You hadn't had a drop. Not that this would have been any excuse for making fun of someone trying to do his job. It's cheeky sods like you who cause all the trouble on the buses."

"I'm sorry if I annoyed you," said Martin, though he realised the man was in no mood to be placated. "I didn't mean to."

"No?" the conductor said, leaning over him and slapping the back of the seat with the flat of his hand. "Well, let me tell you this, mate! If you get on this bus tonight or any other night - and I'm on it and you start that sniggering again, I'll knock your bloody teeth in, do you understand? I'm not going to be laughed at by you nor anyone else either."

Martin kept his eyes straight in front of him.

The man straightened himself up and changing his tone of voice said, "All right, here's your ticket. Give me your money. I've said all I want to say to you," and returned to the lower deck.

Martin sat trembling as he heard the feet clatter down the stairs, He had been afraid something like this would happen one Wednesday. He could not remember having seen the man before but his recollection of Wednesday nights was always a bit hazy. From what he could recall he had been no worse than usual last week and the journey home had passed off all right but the conductor had obviously noticed something. Thank God it had been the last time and nothing like it would happen again that evening! Then he remembered that this had not yet been decided: it still depended on how firmly he conducted himself after reaching his destination in less than a half-hour's time.

The bus had left the streets of the town behind and was in open country now - as open, that is, as the presence of a busy, main road would allow. Beyond the congestion of poles and advertising signs stretched wet fields smothered in doleful mist. The sun which had shone so brightly when he awoke that morning had long since vanished in the clouds and it was impossible to see where it was hiding, no part of the grey sky being any lighter than another. The rain had died off again and no longer pattered against the bus windows or damaged the surface of the syrupy pools lying in paths and gateways beside the road. The road led to the county town, a sprawling city some fifteen miles away, but Martin got off before then, as soon as the houses began to thicken and the urban perimeter was reached. He left the bus without encountering the conductor and stepped on to the pavement outside the Wood Corner Hotel, a bulky, somnolent building that did not wake up until the evening when motorists drove out to it from the city by the score.

On the opposite side of the road from where Martin was standing was the entrance to a tree enclosed lane leading to several villages, the names of which were announced on a leaning white finger post. It was the junction of this lane with the main road and the many trees growing thereabouts that gave the Wood Corner Hotel its name. Martin crossed the road and entered the lane. Moisture was dripping from the arms of the trees interlocking above the roadway and he turned up his raincoat collar for protection against this precipitation though he did not have far to go. He began to run, assuring himself that this was to avoid the wetness yet knowing it was really because he was late and afraid of the consequences. The later he was, the better chance he stood of getting his own way yet he could not stop his feet from hurrying and despised himself for it.

A short distance down the lane, on the right-hand side, were a pair of large ornamental metal gates beyond which a drive wound through thick conifer trees. to a massive brick building almost hidden from the road. The gates, on which hung a white notice, were the only break in an enclosing ten-foot high wall whose summit was stiff with metal spikes. Martin pushed open the unlocked half of the gates and entered the drive, the raindrops on the metal bars splashing in all directions as the gate swung back with a clang. On the notice, painted in black lettering, were the words, HOLTWOOD, the county mental hospital.

Martin hurried along the drive till the forecourt of the hospital came into view: an empty lawn enclosed on three sides by cliffs of red brick pierced with innumerable small windows, each hemmed in by black iron bars. There were birds on the lawn and on the precipitous roofs but they made no noise. It was almost as if they dared not so fierce was the silence hanging over the hospital in its dank grove, and when he ran up the steps to the front entrance, the echo of his feet ricocheted from one brick cliff to another.

As he pushed open the door Martin was met by the now familiar smell of the hospital, a blending of disinfectant, floor polish and stale cooking, which pervaded most of the small area of the building he knew. There was no-one about as he made his way along the cumbrous, oppressive corridor, whose brick walls had been painted in bright colours and hung with pictures to disguise their prison-like appearance, until he reached a vestibule with a door to a ward at the end of it. Martin turned the knob and stepped inside.

It was a very long room with a number of grey painted doors in the wall on one side and a row of tall sash windows on the other, each window guarded on the outside by the inevitable bars. At the near end of the ward, where he was, stood a stove, bulky and old-fashioned but giving off plenty of heat, round which were several armchairs and other seats. Scattered on a table were magazines and worn looking books. Beyond the stove, stretching to the far end of the ward, was a line of twelve beds, the heads of which were under the windows and the feet just opposite the grey doors, each of which had a spyhole drilled in it at eye level, obviously intended for looking in rather than vice-versa.

It was not an unpleasant room, being warm and very light because of the large windows through which could be seen the dark green boughs of the conifer trees beyond, yet the metal bars and the spyholes and something else, more easily felt than seen, created an uneasiness that Martin felt as strongly today as he had done on first entering the ward two months ago. There was not a soul to be seen.

As the door swung to, however, a figure came out of a small dispensary just inside the ward. It was a stout man in his fifties, wearing a white jacket over a navy waistcoat and trousers. His genial features seemed composed entirely of circles; round face, round cheeks, round nose, round chin, and all the circles squeezed together as his mouth stretched into a smile.

"Hello, Martin!" he said. "What's happened to you today? I began to think you weren't coming."

"I missed the bus."

"That won't do, my lad!" the man replied. "What would have happened if you'd been too late? You'd have missed your weekly tot of National Health gin and you wouldn't have liked that, would you?"

"I am too late, aren't I, Mr Clement?" Martin asked. "You know how long it takes with me."

"I don't think so," the man said, looking at his watch. 'It's only just turned two. If you'd been half-an-hour later we might have had to call it off but you've just arrived in the nick of time, as the saying goes. Wait here while I go and measure you a glass."

Martin's heart sank as he watched him disappear into the dispensary though he realised it was his own fault. If he had stuck to his plan and made himself properly late this situation would not have occurred. Now he had the far more difficult task of talking himself out of it.

Mr Clement returned a moment or two later with a medicine glass containing a few drops of colourless liquid.

"Here you are then, Martin! Knock it back! Down the hatch! Cheerio!" He held out the glass confidently, still smiling.

Martin looked at the glass a moment, then turned away.

"No," he said.

"What's that?" asked Mr Clement, surprised.

"I don't want it."

Mr Clement's smile had not shrunk a fraction but something had frozen behind it. Martin had often wondered what the real Mr Clement was like behind the smiling mask. As a male nurse, no doubt called upon to deal with intractable or violent mental patients, he must have a different side to his character from the avuncular one he showed to Martin, and this less amiable side was now apparent in his eyes, which stared at Martin as if sizing him up as a potential adversary.

"Don't tell me you are going teetotal, lad!" he joked. "I thought you liked taking your Wednesday nip! Come on, Martin! Drink it up, there's a good lad!"

"No, I'm sorry, Mr Clement. I don't want to any more. I don't, please."

"Now look here, Martin! The stuff in this glass costs money, don't forget. It's been diluted so I can't put it back in the bottle, can I? You don't want me to chuck it away." He gave a laugh. "Think what it would cost the National Health!"

"I'm sorry"

"Besides, I've got my job to do. The doctor told me to give you this as soon as you arrived and I have to do what he says. That's what I'm here for. You don't want me to get the sack, do you?"

"No."

"Then drink it up like a good lad' Here!"

He held out the glass in front of Martin, who backed away from it without taking his eyes off the liquid moving quietly in the glass. How could that small drop of stuff, as ordinary and harmless looking as water, have such an effect on a person, distorting his senses and imposing such frightful images on his mind! No! He would not drink it and go through that nightmare again!

"I can't, Mr Clement," he said. "I can't any more. You don't know what it's like - how bad it is."

The Trip Back

The smile went from Mr Clement's face as swiftly as chalk wiped from a blackboard. "I don't propose to waste time arguing with you," he said, coldly. "If you didn't like the treatment, you shouldn't have started it in the first place. It was your choice, remember? But now that you've started, it's up to you to see it through. You can't just stop and start when you feel like it. You've got to give it a chance to work. No-one told you it was going to be quick or easy. Come on, Martin! Be sensible. Drink it up!"

Martin went over to a chair by the stove and sat down. How much longer could he hold out? Obviously no matter what he said, Mr Clement was not going to leave him alone till he had emptied the glass. The alternative was to get up and walk out but this was the sort of defiant, independent action of which he had never been capable: besides, he was not sure that he wanted to break with the hospital completely. He might still need their help. Unable to do one thing or the other, Martin just sat there, covering his face with his hands.

He heard Mr Clement put down the glass and sit beside him. An arm went round his shoulders and a voice spoke to him gently.

"You've heard me talk about Wes, my youngest boy, haven't you, Martin?" Mr Clement said. "He's the same age as you and something like you to look at. Wes's got that same sandy-coloured hair and he's a bit on the skinny side like you are. Mrs Clement keeps trying to fatten him up, as she puts it, but he doesn't fill out much - not like his father! Now, having a boy of my own, just like you, you don't think I'd ask you do to something I wouldn't ask him to do? If I thought this treatment would do him good - as I know it will do you good - I wouldn't hesitate to persuade him. I'd tell him to keep on with it till he was better. Don't you see, Martin? I'm on your side?"

Martin did not answer but had got control of himself by now. He had uncovered his face and was quite composed his eyes on the glass and what it contained and he knew that despite all the promises he had made to himself that day, he was going to drink it.

"I tell you what," said Mr Clement, sensing that Martin was about to capitulate. "If you drink it up, I'll arrange for a message to be left at reception for Dr Fletcher to come along and see you the minute he arrives, which shouldn't be long now."

Still Martin was not saying anything.

"If he comes and sees you right away, the stuff won't have had a chance to work and you'll be able to have a talk with him before anything happens. If he thinks you should be taken off the treatment, you may not have to come next Wednesday and I shan't have to make you do something you don't want to do. Nothing could be fairer than that, could it?"

"No," Martin said, at last.

Mr Clement rose and picked up the glass. "Here it is then, my lucky lad!" he said with a chuckle. "For the last time of asking! Down the Hatch!"

Martin swallowed the liquid which was as tasteless as it was colourless. It was all over now and his first reaction was relief that there would be no more arguing. The drug was inside him and after several previous doses he knew what to expect: then despondency set in, not at the thought of the ordeal to come but at the recollection that he had been beaten again. He sensed that if he could just get his own way for once, if he could just get the better of someone like Mr Higlis or the bus conductor or Mr Clement, this would do him a hundred times more good than any substance in a medicine glass or any treatment he was likely to receive in this place.

After patting him on the back, Mr Clement left the ward to leave a message at reception, as promised, and on his return, disappeared into the dispensary without speaking or even glancing in Martin's direction. "Yes, you are no longer interested in me now that you've made me do what you wanted!" thought Martin bitterly, still smarting from his defeat. He picked up a magazine from the ancient heap on the table but found he had seen it before and tossed it back on top of the others, and he did not want to read anyway. He had to think about what he was going to say to the doctor when he arrived.

His relationship with Dr Fletcher was ambiguous. When he was himself, he did not like him particularly but when under the influence of the drug he almost worshiped him. To see the doctor smile at him then or use his name was to feel a thrill that he found inexplicable when the effects of the drug had worn off and he was

The Trip Back

himself again. He knew very little about him apart from the fact that he lived nearby and had a general practice in the city: his special interest lay in psychiatry and he visited Holtwood three afternoons a week from half-past two until it was time for him to leave to take evening surgery. He was still young, probably just over thirty, and his boyishly thick hair had a habit of flopping over his forehead as he bent down to write notes in his book.

Martin wondered how difficult it would be to persuade the doctor to release him from the treatment. Despite the link between them when the drug was doing its work, he knew Dr Fletcher had not much interest in him personally. To him he was just another guinea pig. It was the drug that really fascinated him. He would question Martin about what it was like to be under its spell, whether his body seemed to alter, whether he was projected back in time and if so, how far back, and whether he saw visions of things he could not possibly have known from his own experience, things belonging to a different era of time. Sometimes, when the drug was not working well, Martin was tempted to invent experiences to please him though, equally, at other times he was tempted to ask the doctor, "If you are so interested, why don't you try it yourself?". He knew the answer to this now. The effects of the drug were so erratic that to take it involved a serious risk to one's mental condition. They had not told him this when he started the treatment, of course. They had said the drug was a new one and that some people found it pleasant. "Pleasant!" thought Martin. His life had been made wretched because of it. He had gone to them with a problem and they had given him a dozen more: the trembling, the burning, the stomach turning, the voice nagging inside his head, the fear waking with him each morning.

Although it was only eight weeks since he started the drug, he was already finding it hard to remember what life had been like before then. He remembered how on that morning after he had first taken the drug the world looked as if he were seeing it through a distorting mirror. The objects he touched no longer felt the same nor did he have the same discipline over his body, which shivered, sweated or trembled for no reason he could think of, and for the first time he became aware of walls and ceilings closing in on him, making him want to escape outside. At first he had been alarmed by these things; then he had found he could control them by keeping busy, by occupying his mind, and when he realised they all emanated from his mind, it was then that he began to fear he was going crazy. He was still convinced that unless he broke off the treatment this was what would happen.

He would have to go carefully, of course. He could not afford to offend Dr Fletcher in case the effects of the drug did not wear off and he had to return to him for help. It was ironic that the person from whom he wanted to escape was the same person on whom he had come to depend so much for his morale during these past weeks. An adverse word from the doctor put him in a heart-thumping panic and an encouraging word gave him enough confidence to last several days. The important thing was to convince Dr Fletcher that the treatment was not just failing to help but was actually making him worse. This was nothing less than the truth yet Martin realised he must not over-emphasise the bad effects or the doctor might suggest an alternative to calling off the treatment. Martin gripped the arm of the chair at the thought of what this alternative would be. He surveyed the ward with its row of beds, barred windows and grey doors with their spy-holes and gave a shudder. No! He would never let them talk him into becoming a full-time patient in this place, not matter how ill or desperate he became!

The ward door opened and Dr Fletcher came in carrying a folder under his arm. He must have seen Martin but did not walk towards him or give any sign of recognising him. Instead he walked over to the dispensary where Mr Clement had appeared at the entrance on hearing the door go, and the two men stood talking together for several moments. Because their voices were dropped and they had their backs to him Martin knew they were talking about him; it was one of the things he hated about this place: the way people talked about you at a distance in whispers. The hospital was full of whispers and side glances and mysterious eyes appearing at spy-holes. He knew of no greater relief than to escape from it into the outside world each Wednesday night.

The two stopped talking and Dr Fletcher came over to him smiling.

"Good afternoon, Martin. Mr Clement tells me you didn't want to take the LSD this afternoon."

Martin got up. "Yes, that's right," he said.

"Why was that?"

Martin's answer was not the diplomatic one he had intended. "Because it's making me ill and I don't want to take it any more," he blurted.

Dr Fletcher's smile dimmed a little but did not disappear. "But you did take it?"

"Yes."

"At what time was that?"

"About twenty-five past two."

The doctor looked at his wristwatch. "Only ten minutes ago. That means nothing will be happening for some time yet. You were late this afternoon. If you remember, I asked you to get here as early as possible. It's advisable for me to be with you as long as I can while the drug is doing its work. "You know I have to leave here at five to get back for evening surgery."

"Yes," said Martin, "As I was late I didn't think I would have to take the LSD this afternoon."

"And Mr Clement persuaded you? He is very conscientious." Dr Fletcher tapped Martin's shoulder. "Let's go into the dispensary for a chat. It will be warmer and more private there."

He led the way into the small room opening off the ward and spoke to Mr Clement who was sitting at a table, writing. "We shall be needing this room for ten minutes or so" he said. "Do you think you could find something else to do for a bit?" Mr Clement nodded, put his pen and paper in a drawer and went outside, closing the door behind him. It was the only one in the ward without a spy-hole.

The dispensary was lined with medicine bottles and jars an open shelves or behind glass-fronted cabinets and apart from the table there was a pair of upright wooden chairs and a small bed covered with a grey blanket and other blankets folded to form a pillow at its head. It was certainly cosier than in the ward, the heat coming from a gas fire set in what had once been an open fireplace. Enclosed by the other hospital buildings, the room would have been poorly lit had it not been roofed entirely with panels of clear glass, which even on this dull afternoon let in ample light. Glancing up through the transparent ceiling Martin could see the heavy clouds still sulking overhead, waiting to release their next formidable shower.

"Would you like to lie down?" asked the doctor, indicating the bed.

"No, I'd rather sit?" said Martin, anxious not to allow this to become another psychiatric interview where the doctor sitting upright seemed to have the advantage over the patient lying down.

"As you please," Dr Fletcher replied, sitting at the table, in the chair vacated by Mr Clement and opening the folder, which contained Martin's file. "Well, now, what's the trouble?"

Martin sat opposite the doctor not knowing quite how to begin.

As usual he was baffled by his ambivalent feelings towards the doctor who seemed so different face to face than the man he recollected at a distance during the week. When they parted on Wednesday evenings, Martin was in the throes of an admiration for the doctor that lingered on until the time came for him to return to the hospital the next week. He remembered him as handsome but now they met again he was puzzled at how ordinary the doctor looked and how indifferent his feelings were towards him. Of course, he realised this idealised image of the doctor resulted from the effects of the drug yet after several weeks the image had become more real than the man himself who sat before him now almost like a stranger.

The doctor was not bad looking. He had a lean well-shaped face though his complexion was pale and his blue eyes were so light that they enhanced the impression of pallor. He was fairly tall with long arms thrusting from the sleeves of his white housecoat and terminating in big long-fingered hands. His thick straight hair, which Martin remembered as golden, was a nondescript khaki colour. There was nothing disagreeable about his appearance but he was scarcely the demi-god of Martin's recollection nor did his unassuming manner suggest that he would want to be regarded as one.

"What are you thinking, Martin? I told you it would be better to lie down. You would find it easier to talk that way." This was the doctor's voice cutting in.

The Trip Back

"I was just thinking what to say," Martin replied, jerking himself into conversation. "I know you've been trying to help me and I don't want to offend you by putting things clumsily. It's just that the treatment's not helping me. In fact, it's making me worse."

"In what way?"

"It's hard to explain. I can't point to any particular part of my body and say that's where it hurts. All I can tell you is that I feel frightened all the time."

"But you were frightened when you came to us, weren't you? you went to see your local doctor about it and he arranged for you to come and see us. Isn't that right?"

"I went to see him about this problem I get at the shop and in other places but it doesn't happen all the time. I can go for weeks and be all right. I wouldn't have come to see you just about that. It's a nuisance that Mr Higlis has got to know about it because he takes advantage of it but I could go on coping with it if necessary. I just used it as an excuse really." The doctor looked at him questioningly. "I'm so tired of being pushed around by everyone. They all do it - Mrs Maling, Mr Higlis, even the bus conductor on the bus today. Miss Cutts - that's the lady I work with at the shop - tells me I ought to stand up for myself but I can't. I mean to but when the time comes, I give in as usual. I've read how doctors, psychiatrists I mean, can transform people - make them confident and successful - and that's what I wanted to happen to me."

"Writers tend to exaggerate what can by achieved by psychiatry," Dr Fletcher said with a smile. "I wouldn't believe all you read on that subject. It can help people by uncovering the source of their insecurity but what happens after that depends very much on them. We don't wave a magic wand and change people overnight."

"I would like to overcome this fear I get," said Martin, who had only been half listening, "but there's more to it than that. I also want to get rid of this feeling that I must always give in to other people when they tell me what to do."

"Had it occurred to you that the two might be connected?" asked the doctor. "I'm fairly certain that if we could find out what causes the fear we would be well on the way to solving your other problem too. It's possible that when you were younger you had some unpleasant experience, something to do with a corner, and this has been nagging away at you ever since. It takes its most obvious form when you get one of these panics but as long as it goes on festering inside it can undermine your confidence generally. Your natural aggressive instinct - the urge to stand up for yourself, as you put it - which we all have has in your case been blocked by this suppressed fear."

The doctor paused to push back the inevitable dropping forelock, then looked directly at Martin for the first time that interview. "Do you remember having had such an experience as I've mentioned when you were a child - while playing with other children perhaps, or climbing the stairs in the dark?"

"No, you've asked me about that before and I've thought about it a lot but I can't remember anything unpleasant like that happening."

"It's unlikely that you would," the doctor said, "or this treatment wouldn't have been necessary. Whatever it was, it's now locked away inside your mind and it's here that the LSD is so important because it can project a person back in time as you yourself have already discovered. Because it can take you back, virtually make a child of you again, it enables you to relive certain childhood experiences that may have had a harmful effect psychologically. By bringing such experiences into the open and confronting them, a person can remove the fears and anxieties they created. Do you see what I mean?"

"Yes, I suppose so, but it can't be as easy as that surely? A person's childhood goes on for months and years. The effects of the drug only last a few hours. One might go on taking it for years and years without discovering the particular incident that was the cause of the trouble. It could be an endless task."

"No, it's not as difficult as you think because such experiences are what is known as emotionally charged and are more likely to come to the surface that the hundred and one ordinary incidents of life that passed off pleasantly and were forgotten. I'm sure that if we pursue this treatment we shall discover the cause of your trouble, Martin, but I simply can't promise how long it will take. It could happen this afternoon. It might go on for several months. What do you say? Do you still want to break off the treatment?"

Martin wasn't ready to answer a direct question of this kind. "As I told you," he repeated clumsily, "its making me ill."

"To a certain extent this is inevitable. The nearer we get to what's troubling you, the more it wants to resist. It doesn't want to be remembered. It doesn't want to be brought into the open and it hits back in whatever way it can. It would be fair to say that with this kind of treatment you may have to get worse before you start getting better. Of course, I can't make you continue with the treatment if you don't want to. You came here as a voluntary patient and you have the right to withdraw any time you want to though I would regard it as most unwise of you to do so."

There was a silence as the doctor waited for Martin to answer. The rain had begun falling again and the drops pattering on the glass roof provided a percussive background to the soft hissing of the gas fire in the grate. Dr Fletcher drew out a pencil from his breast pocket and began tapping the table with it.

Martin knew there was only one answer to give. He could not go on as he had been these past weeks, trying to behave normally when nothing seemed normal any more, nor could he face the ordeal of another Wednesday after this one. Though he wanted to avoid saying too much, he realised he would have to be more explicit about wanting to give up the treatment.

"When I came to see you eight weeks ago I had a problem which you know about," he began slowly. "I cannot deny that but otherwise I was all right. Then I had the LSD and nothing was the same any more. When I woke up that first morning it was as if someone had put one of those glass domes over the top of me like they put over food on counters. Everything seemed blurred and cut off by the glass. I stood up and for no reason at all began to tremble and the bedroom, which had seemed so ordinary before, began to close in on me, making me feel I couldn't breathe. I opened the window and pushed my head into the open and the noise of the people and the traffic sounded funny as if they were a long way off instead of close to just as if the glass were shutting out the noise."

The words were tumbling out now. "I don't know how I kept going really" Martin said. "Even a simple action like lifting a teacup seemed difficult and somehow frightening. It was being afraid that was the worst part. Chairs and coats on hangers and any ordinary thing you might mention and the shadows they cast suddenly made me feel nervous though I couldn't tell you why. I was just being afraid for no reason at all. I told you about it, I think, when I came to see you the next Wednesday."

"Yes," said the doctor, "but not quite as graphically as you have done now."

"I know, but I was so keen to get on with the treatment that I didn't want to say anything that might put you off. I still had this idea that it would make a new man of me and that soon I would be surprising everyone at how strong I was. It wasn't until I'd been taking the LSD for several weeks that I began to have doubts about whether it was doing me any good. It was the fear I was finding most difficult to control. You see, it wasn't a meaningless fear any more. It had got a reason. I was afraid I was going mad. A voice started up inside my brain which keeps on at me all the time, telling me I am going out of my mind. It's the last thing I hear when I go to sleep at night and the first thing I hear in the morning. I can't shut it up"

"You are foolish to upset yourself by this sort of thing, Martin," the doctor said, drawing two parallel lines on the cover of the folder. "You are not going mad. Madness and neurosis, which is what you've got, are two entirely different things, they are like the lines on this paper. They run parallel. They do not connect."

Martin felt his usual relief at this reassurance but knew from past experience it would not last long and this time he was not prepared to be persuaded. "It's no use," he said. "Even if I wanted to continue the treatment I couldn't. I can't be sure of keeping a grip on myself any more."

The doctor thought for a moment, then turned away from Martin and studied the folder. He seemed to use this action to avoid looking into Martin's face.

"Would you like to come in for a while?" he asked after a long wait.

For a moment or two everything in the room sounded louder: the raindrops hammered on the glass roof, the gas fire roared in the grate. Martin's ears seemed battered by the noise. So he had been right all along! He was going mad! Otherwise why would the doctor want him to come into this place with its prison walls and iron bars? It was his fear and that voice in his brain that had been telling the truth! The doctor's reassurances had been lies!

"What do you mean?" He was surprised at how calm his voice sounded.

"Would you like to come into the hospital for a few weeks as an in-patient?" replied Dr Fletcher, still gazing at the folder.

"I couldn't do that," Martin said.

"Why not?"

"Because I...because I would have to tell everyone. People would know."

"Why should that trouble you? No-one has objected to your coming here as an out-patient, have they? What's the difference?"

"I haven't told anyone."

For the first time that afternoon the doctor looked at Martin with a gleam of the interest he had shown when Martin was a new patient and the case was still a fresh one.

"Do you mean to say you have told no-one about coming here on Wednesdays?" he said. "Surely you must have told someone - the woman you lodge with, Mrs Maling?"

"No, I didn't want anyone to know."

Dr Fletcher looked sharply at Martin to make sure he was telling the truth, then returned to the folder.

"I think you ought to tell someone," he said quietly.

"Is it necessary?" Martin asked.

The doctor looked annoyed for a moment. "It's advisable that someone should know where you are and that you are undergoing treatment. Obviously if you decide to come in they will have to know but that's nothing to be ashamed of. I know this sort of place had a bad reputation at one time but it's not like that any more. You've seen for yourself what it's like. More and more people are coming here of their own free will for treatment."

Martin thought of what Miss Cutts had said to him that morning about Mr Higlis: "He ought to be in Holtwood along with all the other loonies." It was this remark that had pulled him back from confiding in her. He thought, too, of the people in the street where he lived and of how they would say of someone who did not fit into the pattern: "He'll finish up in Holtwood one day." Or of their silence and exchanged glances when it was reported that someone had been taken to Holtwood. Oh, yes! He knew what the reputation of Holtwood was like and no amount of pretty pictures or bright-coloured paint on the walls would wash that away!

"I don't want to come in, thank you, doctor," he said firmly. He was tired now, tired of explaining and arguing and giving in and paradoxically the tiredness gave him a strength that nothing else would have done. "I want to end the treatment. I don't want to come here again."

Dr Fletcher pushed back his hair from his forehead, then closed the folder with a snap. "In that case there's no point in discussing the matter further," he said. "Personally, I think you are making a mistake but I can't force you to continue if you don't want to."

His voice sounded brusque but he was not angry. Martin had realised for a couple of weeks that the doctor was losing interest as each session became a repetition of the previous one with no developments to sustain his interest. Martin suspected that the doctor was probably glad to be getting rid of a dull patient.

Lifting the cuff of his white coat, Dr Fletcher glanced at his watch. I'll have several other calls to make in the hospital before I return to you," he said, getting to his feet. "When the drug starts to work you know what to do?"

Martin said, "Yes," got up and followed by the doctor went into the ward, where, Mr Clement was ostentatiously tidying up though all he really wanted was to get back into his snug dispensary again. After the inevitable whispered conversation with his watchdog, Dr Fletcher left the ward and Mr Clement returned to sentry duty in the dispensary, where he began reading a sports paper, occasionally glancing at Martin, who had returned to his seat by the stove.

The doctor's invitation to him to become an in-patient had shaken Martin who felt he now had no illusions about the treatment and the effect it was having on him. Obviously something must have gone wrong or the doctor would not have wanted him to move into the hospital. There had been no suggestion when he started the treatment that he would eventually have to become a full-time patient otherwise he would have rejected it from the outset.

He glanced at the bleak sinister ward with its barred windows and spyholes and knew he could not admit himself to such a place. Sometimes he had caught a glimpse of the occupants of the ward, unsmiling men whom he could not help regarding as prisoners and he could not allow himself to become one of their number. On one occasion he had asked Mr Clement what they did during the afternoon, when the ward was empty, and was told "O.T.", which a further explanation had revealed to be short for "Occupational Therapy". Martin knew that no amount of therapy could sustain him were he to give in and join them.

The thought flashed across his mind that if he were going to escape now was the time to do so while he still had the chance. The door was only a short distance from where he was sitting and Mr Clement, who had put on a pair of glasses, appeared to be absorbed in his newspaper just inside the dispensary. Before he knew what was happening, Martin could be out of the ward and halfway up the corridor to the main entrance with no-one to stop him. His hands reached out for his raincoat, slung across the back of an adjoining chair and he quietly got to his feet, ready to make his surprise dash to the door. Then he remembered! How could he run? How could he get away? He had emptied the glass, the drug was inside him and he was its prisoner until it was ready to let him go!

3. EVENING

The light was going. It was the time of year when the days were getting shorter, of course, but the gloomy weather made the dusk come earlier. Soon there were so many shadows in the hospital grounds that the trees seemed to have formed an unbroken dark wall enclosing the building. Inside the ward there was light spilling through the doorway of the dispensary where Mr Clement had switched on an electric lamp to continue reading his paper but the rest of the ward was filled with a trembling greyness that was neither light nor dark. Eventually Mr Clement remembered his duties and walked along the ward, switching on a light here and there: the effect of this was to extinguish the surviving pallor beyond the windows and make the outside world look even darker than it was.

He came over to Martin with the smile of a friend on his mouth and the searching look of a warder in his eyes. "Nothing happening yet?" he asked, creasing his face into genial curves. "You are a slowcoach aren't you?" He laughed. "I've never known anyone as slow to react as you are." He leaned over Martin in a fatherly way till their faces almost touched, his eyes still searching: then satisfied that indeed nothing was happening, squeezed Martin's shoulder and returned to his perch in the dispensary.

Not long afterwards Dr Fletcher returned to the ward, his folder under his arm, and walked across to Martin. He said, "You oughtn't to be out here any longer," adding, with a gesture towards the row of doors with spyholes, "Let's go into one of the cubicles."

The doctor called them cubicles. To Martin they looked and were cells. Each was small and narrow with a thick door and massive walls and a single high-up window, inevitably stiff with bars. The doctor opened one of the doors for Martin to enter and followed him inside. There was an electric light bulb a long way above for what the cell lacked in floor space it made up for in height. The only furnishings were a chair, a narrow bed with a mattress, pillow and pile of blankets on it and beside the top of the bed, a small table on which unexpectedly stood an ashtray, the only extravagance in the room. Dr Fletcher picked up the chair and carried it to the table on which he placed the folder. Martin meanwhile took off his shoes but not his jacket or any other clothing and got on the bed, where he lay flat on his back with his head on the pillow. He pulled a couple of blankets over him because it soon got cold in the cell. The doctor, after positioning his chair so that he looked directly down on Martin's face, opened the folder.

"I've been reading your report from last week," he said. "You don't seem to have had much of a reaction."

He was referring to the report that Martin sent him after each Wednesday session in which he had to explain all that he remembered of it, enabling the doctor to compare it with his own observations. Martin wrote the report on Thursday evenings right under the eyes of Mrs Maling who thought he was sending a letter to his parents, and posted it to the hospital the next day.

"No, it was rotten. Having only half a reaction is worse than having a proper one. I got awful flatulence. My stomach felt all blown out."

"Did you suffer from that when you were a child?"

Martin felt a sudden irritation. Whatever one said to the doctor he always tried to relate it in some way to one's past, finding significance in a commonplace remark or as now in a symptom that everyone had at some time or other such as flatulence.

"No," he replied. "Not that I can recall."

"The reason your reaction was unsatisfactory last week was probably because we cut down on the dosage after you complained of not feeling well. We gave you just about as small a dose as we could and the result was, as you say, not very successful. You are back on the usual dose this week."

Dr Fletcher ran his finger down the report. "I see you mention Doris several times. Who is she?"

"She's Mrs Maling's daughter. She's married now and gone away. I used to play with her a lot when I was small. My parents lived next door to Mrs Maling before my father had to move north because of his job."

"Is she the same age as you?"

"No, three or four years older. I can't remember exactly."

"Several times last Wednesday when Doris appears to have been very much in your mind, you kept making a sort of smacking noise with your lips as if you were blowing kisses or actually kissing someone. Does this mean anything?"

For a moment Martin smelled a whiff of warm timber and creosote. His father's garden shed was redolent of it on hot summer's days with the sun searing the woodwork. There were other smells, too, of strings of onions hanging on the walls and fertiliser bags and black bulb fibre. Before him Martin could see Doris, a small girl in a cotton dress standing with her eyes shut and her lips puckered up, waiting for him to kiss her. It was their kissing game, which they used to play in the shed, a naive imitation of what they believed adults to do when they made love.

Martin told the doctor how he and Doris used to play at kissing, describing their relationship in detail, more for something to say than anything else for he felt under an obligation to keep his interrogator occupied. He knew when a subject was unimportant because he could talk about it easily. When the doctor was probing where it hurt, he tried to veer off the subject or said as little as he could though he guiltily realised that this was the wrong thing to do if the treatment were to succeed. Afterwards he would wonder why a particular apparently unimportant incident should have hurt so much to discuss or why a face suddenly recollected from the past should cause a flash of fear.

He was rambling on about Doris and could see Dr Fletcher trying to hide a yawn. "I'm sorry," the doctor said, realising that Martin had noticed. "I have a young child. It's got teething trouble and keeps us awake at night."

The yawn and the explanation for it went a little way towards humanising the doctor whom Martin now knew to be a family man. He wondered whether he lived in one of those villas in the

The Trip Back

main road near the hospital where the gardens were ostentatiously tidy and over-filled with showy flowers and bushes. The doctor had once told him that gardening was an admirable form of "O.T." and from the tone of his voice it was obvious that he must be an enthusiast himself. Poor Dr Fletcher! thought Martin, contending with neurosis and insanity during the day and trying to banish them from his mind by gardening in his spare time!

"As you are still getting no reaction, I'm going to leave you for a while," Dr Fletcher said, by now as uninterested in Doris and the kissing game as Martin was. "I have calls to make in some of the other wards. Stay here and I'll come back as soon as I can," whereupon he got up and went out.

On his own again Martin stared at the ceiling and thought about Mrs Maling, Mr Higlis and Miss Cutts and wondered what they would think if they could see him now, lying on a bed in Holtwood County Mental Hospital where the loonies were. He thought of what had happened during the day: Mrs Maling in tears at breakfast, the race to the shop because she had made him late, Mr Higlis's unpleasantness, the fainting episode on the landing at the shop, Miss Cutts's kindness, the encounter with the aggressive bus conductor, the argument with Mr Clement over the LSD, the rain, the wet trees, the fading light and now the cell, the end of his journey.

The cell! He felt sort of peaceful as the roll of people he had met and incidents that had happened during the day quietly unwound in his mind like a cinè film, all moving pictures and no sound unless he wanted to switch on with his ears, which he did not feel particularly disposed to do. All pictures! It was cosy under the blankets though he wished he were not wearing his trousers because they would get creased and look untidy when the time came to go home.

Home! All day he had been waiting for the night to come so that he could go safely home and put Wednesday behind him but it did not seem to matter any more He was tucked up comfortably in bed and Mummy would be coming in soon to see that he was all right and kiss him goodnight before turning off the light.

As he stared upwards he could feel the light teasing his eyes from behind the metal grille protecting the bulb on the ceiling. The bars interrupted the light and cast a web of shadows over the cell and the web kept opening and shutting or so it seemed. The bricks in the wall were moving, too, gliding round the cell in horizontal bands till Martin was surrounded by a network of opening and shutting moving lines. The only static point was the spyhole in the door, unobstructed by an onlooker's eye and admitting a halfpenny of light from the ward beyond.

He focused his eye on this bright coin and watched it grow bigger till it shone like a sun, wiping away the pattern of moving lines with its cleansing light. Its edges flared into shapes like ragged petals, then each petal dropped off to form a separate brilliance poised round the main orb, sparkling and flashing. It was most beautiful and Martin felt exhilarated by what he saw.

When the radiance began to fade his eyes tried hard to retain it but the sun shrank slowly till it became a halfpenny spyhole again and the cell was as it had been, cold, empty and still. Martin turned over on his side, feeling puzzled though not sure why. Looking at his wristwatch he saw that nearly fifteen minutes had gone by since he had been left on his own and wondered where he had been all that time and what he had been thinking. There had been lights and shapes but had they been real or had he been asleep and dreaming? He giggled and this, if nothing else, answered his questions. The LSD was beginning to work and giggling was one of its symptoms. He would be doing a good deal of it from now on.

Oh, God! Why didn't the doctor come? Why did he have to waste time talking to other people? Martin felt angry but could not stop himself from giggling and this made him angrier still. He hit the wall with his clenched hand and feeling no pain, was elated to see drops of blood appearing on his knuckles. The drops were like little flowers growing out of his flesh, their red petals opening as the blood seeped over the skin.

Petals! Hadn't he been thinking about petals only a moment or two ago? At the back of his mind he recalled that the doctor had told him to take note of images that repeated themselves because this might have significance, as he put it, and he groped to remember what the petals were, but soon he was giggling again and could remember nothing and was going off again who knows where.

The Trip Back

He had been contemplating his knuckles, wondering where the blood had come from, then looking around saw the entire room was filling up with a flickering red light, the reflection of a crimson flood forming on the floor beneath him. The tide rose slowly over the chair, the table, the bed and himself until they were all like objects at the bottom of a sea while overhead the light on the ceiling shone through the translucent water with a weird roseate glow. He ought to have found himself drenched or gasping for breath, thus inundated, but experienced neither sensation, only an agreeable relaxation floating in the warm ruby-coloured depths. Indeed he was almost sorry when after an interval of uncertain duration the flood began to subside, taking the colour with it, and the harsh white light of the electric bulb reappeared, revealing the cell to be dry and unstained and as grey and cheerless as ever. Everything was so quiet that his wristwatch seemed to tick like thunder.

He stared at the lumps made by his feet under the blankets at the bottom of the bed and at the solid walls around him and the thick door with a spyhole in it, all as they had been before. Before what? he asked himself. Had his mind drifted off again and if so, where and for how long? Oh, how he wished the doctor would come! It was not that he was afraid, he simply wanted someone to show an interest in him and hear what he had to say. It was unkind to leave a child all on his own like this.

Martin was aware that something was happening to his body. The first time it had happened he had been alarmed but now he had got used to it and regarded it more with curiosity than fear. His arms, his legs, his whole frame had shrunk until he was the size of a small child and the bed felt almost too big for him. Even his head rested smaller on the pillow. His arms felt so tiny that he could not resist holding them up to the light for examination but found them no different from usual to look at. Pushing aside the blankets, he raised his legs like a baby lying on its back and saw them, too, to be of their normal dimensions though they felt small: indeed, were small as far as everything but appearance was concerned.

Having adopted this infantile posture he went on to do what appeared to be the most obvious thing which was to wave his arms and kick his legs in the air, giggling as he did so. It was at this moment that the door opened and Dr Fletcher returned.

"What's all this about?" he asked with a mock serious look on his face.

Martin lowered his arms and legs, curled himself up and turned his face to the wall. "I'm not speaking to you," he said.

The doctor picked up the blankets, which had half fallen on the floor, and tidily tucked them over Martin. "Why not?" he said, sitting down beside the bed with his notebook and folder on his knee and fountain pen in his hand. "What have I done?"

"You went away and didn't come back."

"I'm back now," the doctor replied pleasantly. "Don't forget I've got other patients to look after besides you."

Martin's heart burned with jealousy though he expressed it merely by giggling.

"Did anything happen while I was away?" asked Dr Fletcher, ignoring the giggling, a symptom with which he was familiar.

However, when Martin did not answer but simply went on giggling, the doctor had to refer to it as a means of encouraging conversation. "What do you find so amusing?" he said. "Can't you tell me about it?"

Martin kept his face to the wall, refusing to share his thoughts or describe the scene now absorbing him. He could see a field where numerous coloured fountains were playing. They kept thrusting unexpectedly through the turf, showering a tinted cascade and then disappearing into the ground and reappearing elsewhere. There was a man in the field and no matter where he stood, a jet would burst under his feet, knocking him over and soaking him with rainbow spray. The poor man ran all over the place but could not escape the fountains and his soakings got more and more hilarious.

"Come on, tell me about it."

"It's so funny," Martin said, unable to resist sharing his experience. "This man can't get away from the fountains. They come up under his feet and he falls over and gets wet." He rolled over on his back, giggling wildly.

"What does the man think about it?" asked the doctor. "Is he cross?"

The Trip Back

Martin looked to see. "No, he's laughing. He thinks it's funny. He keeps pulling funny faces when it happens."

"Have you seen him before?"

"No...No, of course not!"

The doctor was not convinced. "Is it your father?" he asked with heavy casualness.

This time Martin did not merely giggle, he laughed out loud. What a ridiculous thing to say! As if his father would be in a field surrounded by fountains and pulling a face each time he got wet!

"You didn't answer, Martin."

"No, it's not, you daft thing!" Martin snapped, brushing the idea aside. He did not want to think about people like his father when he was enjoying himself so much.

"There's a beautiful building," he went on. "The fountains are in the gardens of a palace, all white and curly with ornamental pillars and doorways." Then he hesitated. The pictures were beginning to fade. "The man has gone now," he said. "I can't see him any more. It's all going: the fountains, the palace, everything. Wait! No, it's gone. All gone!"

Martin looked up for the first time since Dr Fletcher had returned to the cell. "I can hear your pen nib scratching," he said.

"Did I say anything worth taking down?"

"Not really," the doctor replied, pausing in his note taking. "You went on about fountains and palaces. It didn't add up to anything though it all sounded very pleasant from what I could hear of it. How do you feel?"

"All right."

Seeing him for the first time since the drug began to work Martin felt a surge of affection for the doctor, another familiar symptom though one that felt real enough while it lasted. He would not have wanted to be with anyone other than the doctor at that moment and would have liked to be commanded to run or climb or swim so that he could do so magnificently and win the doctor's admiration. At that time there was no-one he idolised more.

"You're staring at me," said Dr Fletcher, who recognised the look on Martin's face and could not help being lightly flattered by it though he was aware of the hold a doctor had over a patient in Martin's condition.

"You're very good-looking," Martin said.

Dr Fletcher laughed. "My wife would be pleased to hear you say so. She is, I think, the only person likely to agree with you."

Martin smiled, pleased at having made his idol laugh, then turned his head away from the doctor. He could feel himself going off again, giggling, image after image flashing across his mind like slides at a magic lantern show, all unhelpful and confused. He did not know where he was or who he was except that he was tiny and wriggling his arms and legs about, but not afraid.

Several minutes went by without he or Dr Fletcher saying anything. The doctor, was hoping Martin would speak first and when he did not, decided to try a little prompting. "Have you been playing in the garden today?" he asked.

Martin nodded unenthusiastically, still giggling.

"What about Doris? Was she with you?"

Martin rolled over flat on his back and thumped the bed with both fists. "I don't want to talk about her," he said, his mouth trembling.

"Why not?"

"Because she wouldn't let me hold Crystal." Martin was obviously close to tears.

"Who's Crystal?"

"She's her best doll, the one she had for her birthday. She said that if I gave her a sweet she'd let me hold Crystal but she didn't." Martin's face creased and tears began to appear.

"Is Doris often unkind to you?"

Martin did not answer. He was crawling through the tall plants at the bottom of the garden to the sanctuary of his den among the golden rod, Michaelmas daisies and delphiniums. There was an odour of green stalks and earth and summer. No-one could see him there, sitting quietly, legs crossed, and he was glad.

"You didn't answer me, Martin."

"I'm hiding."

"Who from?"

Martin giggled and did not answer.

The doctor looked very cold. There was no heating in the cell, a rime of condensation painted the walls and his breath was steamy. Martin was warm enough under the blankets but the doctor was shivering and obviously finding it difficult to write because his fingers were so cold.

"Do you mind if I borrow one of your blankets?" he asked, an instinctive but unnecessary courtesy because Martin was beyond caring and in any case the doctor probably had as much right to a blanket as his patient.

He raised Martin's feet, removed one of the folded grey blankets on which they were resting and put it round his shoulders before re-seating himself beside the bed.

There was another long silence only interrupted by an occasional giggle from Martin.

"You're not being very helpful today," said Dr Fletcher. "I ask you questions but get no answer. How can I help if you don't co-operate?" How can you expect the treatment to work?"

Late.

The doctor's hand went up to his mouth unsuccessfully to hide a yawn. Successively he looked at his wristwatch, tapped the empty page of his notebook with his pen, grappled with his pocket for a handkerchief, wiped his nose and then put the handkerchief back. "Well, Martin?" he said, without much enthusiasm.

The bed on which Martin was lying was moving so fast that he could feel the wind on his face and was aware of the walls streaming past and the ceiling opening above him. He was elated as he soared upwards into the emptiness, leaving behind the doctor's questions and the complications of being himself. No-one could confuse him now as he circled above the cell, looking down on the doctor in his chair with his silly notebook in his hand. To fly was to be free and he could fly! He could soar up above and no-one could catch him and it was all so easy, the easiest thing he had ever done."

Late. Late. Late. Late. Late.

Martin bit his lip. He wished this word would not keep coming back to worry him. Why had it not stayed behind with all the other things he wanted to forget? He was not late. He did not want to be told he was late. He wanted to go on flying serenely as he had done before this word appeared like a cloud in the sky.

It was not so easy to fly now. All the pleasure had gone out of it and neither flapping his arms nor kicking his legs could prevent him from losing height, slowly at first, then faster like a falling stone. There was an upthrust of air as the surface below rose to meet him, tilting up and down as he saw it from different angles and flashing like a sheet of glass. He was completely out of control and nothing now could slow him down or stop him from falling. He was going to smash into that glass surface like a wretched insect against a window pane, and sweat sparkled on his forehead as he gripped the sides of the bed, turned his head away and stiffened his body in expectation of the impact.

When it came - when his body hit the glass - he threw himself violently sideways, his hands protecting his face against the broken flying pieces, and hit his head against Dr Fletcher's knee, knocking the notebook to the floor.

"What was that all about?" asked the doctor, picking up the book. "You didn't seem to be having such a good time that time. Tell me about it."

Martin, aware of the perspiration on his face and the tautness of his body, felt shaken for the first time since the reaction began that afternoon. The effects of the drug could be pleasant or unpleasant or a mixture of both. So far this had promised to be one of the pleasanter sessions. Now he was not so sure.

Late. Late. Late. The word kept pressing against his mind.

"Just a minute," he said, straightening himself out on the bed. "I'm a bit out of breath."

"I'm not surprised with all that kicking and arm flapping you've been doing," said Dr Fletcher with a smile.

Martin did not smile back. He did not like the way this word pursued him or the panic he felt gathering round his heart. Something he was afraid of was stirring inside him and he did not know what it was. Something inside the dark caves of his mind was being unchained.

He looked up at Dr Fletcher for reassurance and immediately froze at what he saw. The doctor's blue eyes slowly detached themselves from their sockets and slid down his cheeks, leaving sticky, silvery trails across the skin. Cracks appeared in the doctor's forehead, down the centre of his nose and across his cheek bones and widened and blackened till his face fell apart, leaving nothing recognisable but the two white eyeballs hanging in the emptiness.

Terrified, Martin turned his head away, pressed his face against the pillow and tried to blot out what he had seen.

"What's wrong?" asked the doctor, interested by Martin's change of mood and more alert than he had been. "Why hide your face like that?"

"Because something has happened to your face! I don't want to look at it!"

"My face is all right," the doctor replied, not without instinctively running his hand down it to make sure, a movement that, fortunately, Martin did not see. "Look at me!"

Martin turned slowly to face him and was relieved that what the doctor said was true though there still seemed to be smudges where the cracks had been. "I'm still afraid," he said. "I don't know what's happening. Why is it so dark?"

"Martin," said the doctor seriously. "You keep muttering a word under your breath. I've been trying to make out what it is. It sounds like "late" or a word like that. Does it mean anything to you?"

"I was late for work this morning" said Martin. "I had to run all the way. That's why I keep saying it."

But it wasn't, was it? It went back much, much further than this morning. He was sitting on the lavatory at home and was so small that his feet scarcely touched the floor. The room looked large because he was a child and the electric light, which was on because it was a dark morning, hung far above his head. Someone was knocking on the door, which he had locked.

"Martin, what have you locked yourself in there for?" It was his mother's voice. "You'll be late for school."

"I can't go," replied Martin miserably.

"Can't go where?" asked Dr Fletcher.

"I want to go to the lavatory but it won't come," said Martin in such a woebegone way that the doctor had a job not to smile.

Martin could hear his mother calling him again. "Please open the door" she said. "It's quarter-to-nine, Martin. Doris has called for you but she can't wait any longer. Can't you go when you get to school?"

"No!" shouted Martin. "I want to go now! I've wanted to go ever since I got up but I can't!" and he started crying. He was very upset at Doris leaving without him. He had never been to school on his own and it was a long walk, much further than he had ever walked alone before.

"Doris won't wait," he told the doctor. "She's gone to school without me."

"You still want to go to the lavatory?" asked Dr Fletcher.

"Yes, I keep pushing but it won't come. I've got to go or else when I get down the road it'll come." He gripped the seat with his small hands and went on trying without success.

More knocking on the door. "Martin, do you realise what time it is?" said his mother. "It's nine o'clock. What's Miss Barber going to say?"

Nine o'clock! The time when the children were gathering in the hall for prayers and here he was still at home! Sometimes when a boy came to school late he had to stand at the front where everyone could see him, until prayers were over. It was horrible!

The thought of such a humiliation happening to him stirred Martin into action. He pulled up his trousers, unlocked the door and threw himself against his mother, who was waiting outside. "Did you go?" she asked.

"No, I couldn't," he said. "And now I'm late and Doris has gone without me."

"Well, it's you're own fault," his mother said. "I told you several times to open the door but you wouldn't. You've been very silly and when you get to school Miss Barber will be cross with you."

"I don't want to go to school," said Martin. "It's too far and too late."

"No, it's not," replied his mother. "You can manage without Doris for once. It's time you got used to going to school on your own. You ought to be able to look after yourself by now. So stop crying, put on your raincoat and get off as quick as you can"'

"Mummy says I've got to go to school on my own," Martin muttered. "She's cross with me."

"So I gathered," said Dr Fletcher. "What's happening now?"

Martin wiped the wetness from his face and looked around. The sun was up but out-of-doors the weather was more dusk than day. There was such a thickness of cloud overhead that it was impossible to tell where the sun was and the street had a wet, gloomy look. Raindrops from the early morning shower hung on the railings and not many doorsteps had been scrubbed, the women doubtless thinking that it would be wasted work with more rain to come.

He ran faster than he had ever done, his legs flying along the pavement. "Late, terribly late!" he hissed at Dr Fletcher. "Must run all the way!" He knew he would eventually have to stop for a rest. He just wanted to get as far as he could before stopping for the first time.

At the bottom of the street he entered Norton Avenue where the houses were bigger and had gardens with lawns and shrubs. As Doris, like everyone else from his street, always crossed to the other side, where there were no houses, only a tall wall, he automatically did the same. He ran under the wall with its crown of broken glass and saw the first landmark flash by: a single yellow brick glaring among the multitudinous red ones in the wall's surface. At the next landmark, the tree with a hole in it, he was so out of breath that he had to stop, clinging to the tree and resting his head on the ledge of the hole formed by a deformity in the bark a few feet above the pavement.

After counting to ten, which was as high as he could go, he ran on but had to stop again only a few yards farther on, at the splash of blue, where someone had once spilt a tin of paint on the pavement. He leaned against the wall, his chest heaving, and thought how silly he had been to waste so much time trying to go to the lavatory when it was obvious now that he had not wanted to go at all. That feeling had vanished and the only thing worrying him now was that he must get to school quickly. There was something reassuring about the yellow brick, the hole in the tree and the blue paint on the pavement because they were measurements of his journey: the more such landmarks he passed, the sooner he would be at school, but his poor legs were trembling after running so hard.

"I can't run any more," he gasped. "My legs are shaking," and the doctor could see they were under the blankets.

Still he did, after a rest, running less quickly than before, and when he next stopped he had reached the "Royal", the cinema where Norton Avenue reached the main street of the town. As he stood under the cinema's unlit neon sign, he felt a sharp pain in his side, which always came when he had run too far or too fast, and his hand went down to rub the place where it hurt.

"What are you doing that for?" asked Dr Fletcher.

"Because it hurts," replied Martin. "I've got the stitch through running. I'll have to wait a bit till it wears off." He lay on the bed panting, still rubbing his side.

After a minute or two the pain settled into a dull feeling that he could bear and he continued running along the main street, weaving among the people on the pavement, mostly women who were disconcerted when he glanced against them or their shopping bags and told him to go carefully or he would hurt himself.

There was an unpleasant rhythmic banging in his ears and the more he ran, the louder it got, like the thumping of a drum. He did not know where the noise was coming from but soon his body was throbbing with the sound, making him feel giddy and confused. The thumping got so loud that he could stand it no longer and rolled to and fro on the bed with his hands over his ears.

The doctor looked at him inquiringly. "What's the matter?" he said.

"It's the banging. Where's it coming from? Can't you make it stop?"

"I can't hear anything," said Dr Fletcher.

Martin listened. The sound was coming from inside him! He put his hand on his chest and was amazed at how his heart was thumping up and down. "Oh, God! It's my heart!" he exclaimed.

The doctor leaned forward and lifted Martin's wrist. "Your pulse is right," he said after a moment or two. "There's nothing to worry about. Carry on. Tell me what's happening now."

Martin was standing in the middle of the bridge linking the dowdier part of the town, where he lived, with the glossier, more prosperous part. The sky was dark and there was no sparkle on the

The Trip Back

river but it was possible to see the hands of the clock on the church tower rising above the rooftops. They were in a position that Martin had never seen them before on his way to or from the school, with both hands level, forming a horizontal line across the face.

"Please, what's the time?" he asked a man walking past.

"Quarter-past-nine," came the reply. "Time you were in school! You're going to cop it, aren't you? Being as late as this."

For the first time since leaving home Martin despaired. He was late, his mother was cross with him and Miss Barber would soon be, too; he had the stitch in his side, his legs were aching, his shirt was sticking to his back because he was sweating so much: everything was against him. He no longer ran but walked along the pavement not attempting to hide that he was crying again. None of the lofty walkers took any notice of him nor did he care.

And so he reached the grocer's shop at the corner of School Road, where his friend, the stag, was leaping from cliff to cliff on the advertising plate on the wall high above the street. Martin looked up at the creature, so confident and brave, soaring through the air against an optimistic blue sky. Its front legs were taut and outstretched with exertion but there was not a flicker of doubt in its eyes that it would fail to reach the other side. Its brown coat and crown of antlers shone. It was indomitable.

As he studied the picture Martin stopped crying. If the stag could jump the chasm without fear, why should he be despondent? The stag had not given in and nor would he. "I'm going to run because of the stag," he said, starting off again. "There's not much farther to go."

"The stag?" said Dr Fletcher, surprised, though he did not press the question after seeing his patient panting as he resumed his journey.

There was a pavement on only one side of School Road and Martin crossed over to it after leaving the main street behind just as Doris would have done. Because of a rise in the land on that side, the pavement got gradually higher above the road, culminating at a height of about nine feet, where it resembled a ledge on the side of a cliff with the walls of the houses rising sheer on one side of the path and the retaining wall dropping sheer to the road on the other. A black metal handrail ran along the edge of the path to prevent people from falling off: sometimes he had seen bigger boys showing off by swinging on the handrail to and fro over the drop while the girls screamed alarm and admiration from the road below. Martin ran along the pavement, watching the road slowly fall away below him and keeping well away from the edge, as Doris had always told him to, though he could not get too close to the houses because their doors opened directly on to the path and people had put out empty milk bottles that got in his way. He met no-one. School Road was a quiet place at that time of the day when all the children were in school, and his tiny footsteps echoed in the empty canyon of the street.

As the vision of the stag began to blur in his mind, his worries returned about what would happen when he got to the school. They said Miss Barber kept a stick in her office and if she did, who else would she use it on but a boy who came to school not just a little late but after the clock's hands had pointed to a quarter-past-nine? He ran faster, hoping that when she saw how tired and out-of-breath he was she would know how hard he had tried to get to school and forgive him for being late. There was hardly any distance to go now. All he had to do was to reach the end of School Road, turn the corner and the school would be right in front of him.

The Corner!

Martin rose up on the bed gripped with alarm. "The corner!" he gasped. "I've got to go round the corner!"

The doctor looked at him sharply. "It's all right," he said in an interested voice. "Nothing's going to hurt you. Don't stop now."

"No, I'm afraid. I don't want to go on.

"You must, Martin," the doctor said, putting his notebook and pen to one side and leaning forward. "This is very important. Please try."

"I can't, I can't!" Martin replied.

The doctor realised that he would have to be cruel. "You haven't any choice," he said harshly. "You've been very silly! You're late for school! You've run all the way from home! If you stop now, you'll only get into more trouble! You've got to go on!"

Martin fell back on the pillow. Yes, he had to go on. Running, running, running! If he went back home his mother would be just as angry with him as Miss Barber. There was no going back, and all the time the corner was getting nearer, that vertical line dividing the seen from the unseen, and he had to keep running though his legs shook and he had that pain in his side again.

The corner! That high wall, the path, the rail, the drop to the road. No escape from it now. But what if he should meet something there? Where could he go with the wall on one side and the drop on the other? How could he get out of its way?

"You've been very naughty and I hope Miss Barber will be cross with you," his mother said.

Bang! Bang! Bang! His heart was battering his ribs again like an animal rampaging in a cage. How could it go on beating like that without bursting? It would burst and he would die! That's what would happen: he would die!

"Would you get a pair of cricket boots from the attic, Martin?"

"Yes, Mr. Higlis," he says. Up the stairs he goes to the top floor, along the corridor, and then the corner at the foot of the attic stairs. The corner! That vertical line again! And what creature behind it in the shadows waiting to capture him? What terrible thing could it be?

Martin writhed on the bed with sweat shining on his face. "Please don't let me die! he cried.

"Don't be silly!" said Dr Fletcher. "You're not going to die. In a few seconds everything will be over. You'll have got round the corner and be at the school."

"Not the corner!" said Martin, but he couldn't stop now. His legs were out of control, thrusting him forward as if he were a passenger in a runaway vehicle.

"You're going to cop it, aren't you, being this late?" said the man on the bridge. Cop it! Naughty! Punish! Stick! the words flashed on an off like captions on a newscaster in his mind. Then he was there, hurtling round the corner in a last spurt to the school: the end house rose above him like a cliff, the handrail swung across in front of him as it cut round the corner, the road gaped below and the thing he feared stepped out of the unknown. They were face to face.

"No!" screamed Martin, and he threw himself off the bed, taking the blankets with him, and fell sprawling on the floor of the cell. "For God's sake, let me go!"

Dr Fletcher dropped on his knees and seized him be the shoulders. "What is it, Martin? What can you see?"

"I don't know," Martin answered, clutching the doctor's legs as if afraid of being swept away. "I don't know."

"Yes, you do!" exclaimed the doctor, gripping him hard. "Tell me what it is!"

Martin sort of whimpered, then looked up and shiveringly said, "It was a monster covered with scales with a big red mouth and – "

"No, it wasn't," the doctor cut in angrily. "That's something you've made up! Tell me what it really was!"

Martin let go of the legs and slid down till his face rested on the doctor's shoes and he lay there saying nothing. He felt the shoes move away and looking up, blurrily saw the doctor open the cell door and click his fingers several times. Almost immediately Mr Clement appeared and the two of them lifted Martin back on the bed.

Mr Clement went out and when he returned, carried a bottle of tablets and a glass of water. "Take these," said the doctor, giving Martin two of the tablets and helping him to hold the glass steady as he washed them down. Mr Clement stood by the door.

After a couple of minutes Martin quietened down apart from a resumption of the giggling, a symptom not to be easily shaken off. Dr Fletcher took Martin's pulse, then without letting go of his wrist, said, "I've got to go now. Its five o'clock and I have to take evening surgery in half-an-hour's time. Do you hear what I'm saying?"

Martin nodded.

"You've had a strong reaction today and I don't think you should go home tonight. I know you probably want to but it would be silly if you're not properly recovered. I'll ask Mr Clement to keep an eye on you and he'll decide whether you ought to go or not. He can if necessary arrange to let your people know where you are. Do you understand?" Martin nodded again and giggled.

"I think we may have stumbled on something today," the doctor continued, "and when you can, I want you to think over what's happened, write down all you can remember and post your report to me as you have done before. It's a pity I have to go but it's unavoidable."

The Trip Back

The doctor looked at his wristwatch. "Of course," he said with a comradely smile that warmed Martin like the sun. "It's really your fault for being so slow getting started." They were so close that Martin half expected the doctor to hug him before leaving but this did not happen and he had to be content with the concern in Dr Fletcher's voice, the interest in his eyes and the smile. It was more than enough.

He felt the hand leave his wrist, there was a murmuring in the corner as instructions were given to Mr Clement, and then the doctor was gone.

Martin's mind wandered off, he could not remember where, and when he next came to, he felt a spongy hand kneading his, looked up and saw the full-moon face of Mr Clement, who had taken the doctor's place in the chair beside the bed.

"Hello," Martin said.

"Hello," came the reply. "How are you feeling"

"All right."

"That's a good lad," said Mr Clement, giving Martin's hand a squeeze. "Aren't you glad now you took my advice?"

Martin vaguely recalled his unsuccessful resistance to taking the LSD and nodded though even in his present comatose state he felt he had been right and that he would be sorry tomorrow to have given in.

"Of course you are," said Mr Clement. "The treatment's doing you good, isn't it?"

Martin did not nod or reply to this question: comatose or not he was not going to concede this point to anyone!

Mr Clement, still pumping Martin's hand, seemed miffed and said, "You don't think Dr Fletcher would put you on this treatment if he thought it was going to do you any harm? Of course not! He's the best doctor in the hospital." Mr Clement realised he might have been indiscreet and added, "The others are very good but they don't have that - you know what I mean - that pleasant way of his."

All the time Mr Clement was keeping his eyes fixed on Martin, two unsmiling points in an otherwise genial expanse of face. Martin, when he was aware of where he was, which was not often, felt like a specimen on glass slide. He didn't try talking but just let Mr Clement chatter on, unable to follow most of what he said.

Eventually Mr Clement withdrew his hands, slapped his knees and rose. "Well," he said, after a final stare, "I think the baby's all right to be left on his own for a while. How would you like a cup of tea, Martin? I'll pop along to the kitchen and get you one. You'd like that, wouldn't you?"

Martin said he would and when Mr Clement went out, lay back on the bed comfortably. He thought mostly of the doctor when he was able, for his mind kept going off and he would suddenly find his eyes focusing on the walls of the cell or the door and wonder where he had been since he last saw them. The race to the school still stuck in his mind but he would think about that later. All he wanted to do now was to relish the echoes of Dr Fletcher's voice and presence. That the doctor had suggested he remain overnight was another matter that he did not particularly want to consider for the time being. It was the warmth the doctor evidently felt for him that preoccupied him now.

Soon Mr Clement returned carrying a heavy white mug filled with dark brown tea almost as thick as its container. "There you are, my lad!" he said, beaming. "The cup that cheers. You can have something to eat later if you want to."

Martin raised himself up and drank the tea rather unsteadily and so Mr Clement helped him hold the mug until it was half empty.

"You know, Martin," he said, resuming his seat by the bed, "as I've said before, there's a remarkable resemblance between you and my boy, Wes. Tell me, do you happen to play football?"

Martin shook his head, drank some more of the tea and then put the mug on the table before lying flat again. He had a feeling Mrs Maling had said something about a football match being on the television that night.

"Wes is very keen on the game," Mr Clement continued. "He plays for Wood Corner - the village just down the road. He's like you, slim-built, but wonderfully light on his feet. It's a treat to see him running circles round the big fellows, who just can't stop him. I go to most of his home matches. Do you watch football?"

"Sometimes," said Martin, finding it exhausting to keep up with Mr Clement and irritating, too, to have him hovering and chattering incessantly. This didn't prevent Martin from giggling from time to time though Mr Clement ignored this as coolly as the doctor had done.

"Oh, I like to get to a football match when I can," Mr Clement went on. "In fact I never miss a Saturday game except when I'm on duty - and even then I sometimes get a few minutes at the game down the road. If the weather's all right, we take some of the patients - the good ones, you know - for a walk. The exercise and fresh air does them good and takes them out of themselves - makes them think outwardly. The men on the gate let us in free. Its very good of them really though we don't stay until the end of match." He paused. "Aren't you going to finish your tea?"

Martin raised himself up again, leaned towards the table and laughed: not a giggle but a genuine laugh this time. When he had put down the mug he had, as result of normally using a cup and saucer, put it right in the middle of the ashtray. "Look," he said to Mr Clement. "Look what I did with the mug! I put it in the ashtray thinking it was a saucer!"

He looked up expecting to find Mr Clement smiling but the face was unresponsive, the eyes cold. Thinking that maybe he had not understood, Martin turned his eyes towards the mug and the ashtray to indicate what he had done and looked up again. "Yes, very funny," Mr Clement replied in a curtly tolerant voice, the tone of which suggested that if Martin wanted to put the mug on top of his head or empty it down his trousers he could do so and nothing would be thought amiss. There was no shared amusement, no feeling of a joke they could both enjoy.

Martin felt a sudden repugnance not just for Mr Clement but for the cell, the ward, the hospital and everything to do with it. He had not put the mug in the ashtray deliberately. It was the sort of thing that anyone might have done who was accustomed to using a cup and saucer. What sort of place was it where a slip like this had to be interpreted as some kind of symptom of his condition - as something to be patiently tolerated or quietly ignored? Martin could feel his mind drifting off again but of one thing he was certain: he was not going to stay in Holtwood Hospital one minute longer than he had to. He was going home that night no matter what Mr Clement or anyone else might do to stop him.

4. NIGHT

Martin had found that the time spent recovering from the LSD was usually the pleasantest part of the experience. He lay back quietly - the tablets given him may have had something to do with this - and dreamily watched the pictures switch on and off on the cinè screen of his mind under the blankets aware that the worst was over.

He assessed the right time to go home by the length of the clear intervals between the fuzzy ones and his ability to think coherently more or less continuously. If the doctor's warning were correct it might take longer to achieve such a condition tonight but this was something that remained to be seen. The fuzziness would not go completely till the morning but it and the giggling became only momentary after an hour or two and instead of coming to after five or ten minutes as he had been doing, wondering where he had been, his absences would last no longer than a few seconds: merely the time it was now taking for an image to flash on and off in his mind.

Some of these images were so bizarre that he often wondered from what secret lockers of his mind they must emerge.

For a few moments he glimpsed a Tudor garden with hedges shaped razor-neat into elaborate balls, cubes and, spirals, and between them, prancing to the music of mysterious instruments, a procession of ostriches dressed in jewels and ornamental cloths. Each of the inelegant birds wore an embroidered cap with a pendant pearl dropping over its forehead and Martin had to smile before they disappeared because they looked so incongruous in such finery and in such a setting.

The last bus left the Wood Corner Hotel at half-past nine and Martin decided to leave it as late as he could - say, quarter-past-nine

- before attempting to get away from the hospital. In the past he had always been ready to leave well before this and had often gone home on earlier buses without trouble apart from hiding his giggling. Primarily, he had to make sure he could convince Mr Clement that he was all right to go and this might not be easy. On some occasions Mr Clements had told him to go back for another half-hour before allowing him to leave and if this were to happen tonight it would be a disaster. By the time the half-hour was up the last bus would have gone and there would be no alternative but to stay overnight, something Martin was determined not to do. However, he still felt it best to defer his departure for for as long he could so that he would be as far recovered as possible when he presented himself to Mr Clement for inspection.

There were more birds now, not live creatures but statues, each consisting of a human form with a bird's head. One of the statues had the head of a hawk wearing a full moon with a snake coiled on it: another had the head of a bird with a long thin beak and this statue wore a crescent moon. More statues appeared with the heads of animals: a lion, a dog and a cow with shapely upswept horns, all surmounted by curious, elaborate headpieces incorporating either a full or crescent moon. Martin felt that he was looking up at them in bright sunlight, seeing them against a beautiful blue sky. As his vision fixed on the hawk's head there was a loud noise like a blast from a trumpet and the bird's eye - for he could only see one side of its face - crumbled into dust, leaving a startling void on its face, and this was disturbing.

Looking at his watch he saw that it was nearly half-past six: time for him to be getting a further visit from Mr Clement, who would ask whether he wanted something to eat. On an earlier visit Martin had said "Yes" out of politeness and had been given two thick slices of bread, a large piece of cake and a dish of flavourless red jelly with custard, none of which he had been able to consume entirely. He had not been hungry anyway. Now, Mr Clement's offer of sustenance was more of a formality than anything else because he knew Martin would certainly refuse.

The next thing to happen would be what appeared to be a social gathering in the room or hall overhead. There was music and much moving about of feet that went on from seven to eight when the movement shifted to the ward outside, signifying that the occupants of the twelve beds who had been with the others upstairs, were turning in. Before they arrived Martin made a point of visiting the lavatory so that he did not have to encounter them when they were still up and about. By the time he left they were all in bed either asleep or trying to sleep and the ward was dark. He felt no urgent need to go to the lavatory at present and decided to embark on his expedition there at half-past seven, which would give him a chance to see how he was progressing and assess his chances of escape.

Human faces appeared from time to time like snapshots in his mind and were so vivid and distinctive that he felt they must belong to real people yet he knew quite well he had never seen any of them before. That man who glanced at him then had a winking face Martin could pick out again in any crowd: that woman with the sad eyes and anxious strand of hair trailing down the side of her pale cheek was equally memorable. For a moment he was aware of a recognisable personality, then the face was gone, leaving an impression behind of someone who lived and breathed, but if these people were strangers, where had they come from and why were they in his mind? It was something that Martin could not understand.

The cell door opened. "All right then?" said Mr Clement. "Want anything to eat?"

"No thanks," said Martin, raising himself up. "Sorry."

"No need to apologise, lad," Mr Clement replied. "I know what hospital food's like. I've had to live with it for twenty years and look what it's done to me!" With a laugh he patted his rotund stomach, then laughed again.

He must either have been satisfied with Martin's condition or have had other things to do because this time he made no attempt to stay and the cell door closed to.

Martin was continuing to get that shrinking sensation, the feeling that his body was smaller than it was and that if, for example, he were to sit on the side of the bed his legs would be too short to touch the floor; but he could observe this condition detachedly now and not become immersed in the re-enactment of a childhood experience as he had done over the race to the school.

The race to the school! The time had come to start thinking about this, to try recalling the details in readiness for his written report to the doctor. There was no doubt, looking back on it now, that it had been an alarming experience, as much when it first happened as when he had re-lived it under the drug only a short time ago. That it had actually happened was beyond doubt. He could remember the episode clearly without artificial prompting though if anyone had asked him about it that morning he would certainly have had difficulty in recalling it. Now, the details were as fresh as if it had happened that very afternoon, which in a sense it had.

He could remember he was wearing shoes with over-long laces which his mother had tied double to prevent them working loose. His long socks had been the ones she had knitted for him and had red bands round the top to match a jersey, which he had also been wearing, with similar bands. All the garments had long been discarded.

The events of that day seemed so near: his wanting to go to the lavatory, his late departure from home, his journey to the school - the first time he had gone there on his own - then his alarm at the prospect of being punished and finally the corner. He clearly remembered reaching the latter but could remember nothing after that. What, if anything, had happened there? Why could he not remember when the rest was so clear? Was the corner the location of the "emotionally charged" incident that the doctor had been talking about that afternoon, which might provide the clue to Martin's fear?

Lying on the bed with his mind moving all the time towards normal, Martin recalled that the first thing he could remember after reaching the corner was being inside the school after finishing his journey. Though it was morning the hall had been in twilight, due to the bad weather, and there had been a ripple of thunder overhead as he presented himself to Miss Barber, the head teacher. She had taken him by both hands and had not been angry, as he had expected, but anxious, kind and consoling.

"Oh, Martin, I'm so glad to see you," she said, or something like that. "We were getting so worried. We thought something must have happened to you, You've never been late before. Miss Milne and I didn't know what to do. It's such a relief to know you're all right."

Her kindness had been unable to dissuade him from crying and she had been obliged to fall back on her standby for all crises.

"If you promise not to cry," she said, "I'll take you into the office and give you a peardrop from the sweet jar. How about that."

Miss Barber's peardrops, sugared, multi-coloured and tangy, were sparingly given by her as a reward for virtue or consolation in distress and were infallible in their effect. Martin had stopped crying.

"That's a good boy," Miss Barber said. "Let's take off your raincoat and then we'll go into the office for that sweet," She paused. "Why, Martin, what on earth have you done to your raincoat? It's all torn."

Martin felt himself go icy under the blankets. His raincoat had been torn!

It had been all right when he left home, he was sure of that. When had it got torn? It was an awful tear, too, almost from top to bottom of the coat. Miss Barber had stitched it together roughly to prevent it from getting worse and had told him to let his mother have a look at it as soon as he got home. This he had done and she had been annoyed because the coat was almost new. She had questioned him - that's right, it was coming back to him now - she had questioned him about how he had torn the coat and he had told her he could not remember, which had made her angrier. She had said he must have been doing something silly or he would have explained how it had got torn but the truth was he had genuinely been unable to remember. If he could have done, he would have owned up and avoided being sent to bed early, which had been his punishment after tea for damaging the coat.

The corner, the torn coat.

Martin thought about them both for a long time but nothing emerged to shed light on either or to link them together and he got tired of thinking, shut his eyes and dozed off for a while. It was not a restful sleep but at least it occupied the time while he was waiting. The next thing he heard was a rumbling above as tables and chairs were moved and many feet walked about overhead, indicating that seven o'clock had arrived and the weekly party or whatever it was, was about to start. Someone began to play a piano and the foot movements became more orderly and rhythmic as the company danced, none too expertly, it seemed, from the heaviness of the steps and the floorboard creaks accompanying them.

Between dances there would be a screeching of chairs as the participants resumed their places and often there was a lull in which a remote voice could be heard though Martin could not tell what it was saying. He wondered whether it might be an entertainer, a comedian, perhaps, telling funny stories, but no-one laughed: laughter was not a sound one associated with Holtwood Hospital. Sometimes the tread of feet would weave a pattern round the ceiling, culminating in a rush, a skidding stampede, as though they were playing party games, but still no laughter, no sound of voices at all, only the piano, the chairs being moved and the feet.

Yet soon a voice would come that Martin half longed to hear, half dreaded. Someone in the room, one of the men patients (so Mr Clement had told him) had a lovely voice and at a certain point during the hour would sing with such a mixture of sweetness and sadness that one hardly knew whether one wanted to hear him or not, so poignant was the sensation. Martin knew that when he was old and all his other memories of Holtwood had gone, he would still remember this man's voice filtering through the gloomy building like a whiff of fragrance in a musty room.

When the moment came and the man began to sing, Martin pulled the blankets over his head and turned on his side, knowing that he was likely to weep and wishing his tears to be private even from the light. He thought of his far-off parents and how shocked they would be if they knew where he was now; of the hopeful child he had been and the ineffectual person he had grown into, and of his ambitions which had so far led nowhere. Then he thought of the singer, the nightingale behind bars, and felt ashamed, remembering how fortunate he was compared with the others in this place. With luck he would be home tonight but for the laughterless company above it might be weeks or months or even years before they were free. This was his last Wednesday but for them the future was a vista of Wednesdays, and when his tears came they were more for his neighbours than himself.

At half-past seven he got off the bed and stood up for the first time since entering the cell that afternoon. He felt as though he had been on the booze with the floor unsteady under his feet though he was in no danger of falling, fortunately. Before going into the ward he walked up and down in the cell in his stockinged feet to get used to moving about, then pushed open the door. The ward was lighted from end to end though no-one was to be seen, Mr Clement being no doubt tucked away in his dispensary, and Martin moved quietly, not wanting to bring him out.

The lavatories were at the far end of the ward in an austere washroom where there was a row of washbasins, a urinal and six WCs, none with a doorknob or lock on the door. There was no chance of anyone at Holtwood locking himself in, either for privacy or for a more sinister reason.

After urinating Martin went to a basin to wash his hands and caught sight of himself in a mirror on the wall, which gave him shock though he should have been prepared for it. His face was deeply flushed as though he had been running hard or sitting over a blazing fire, and his hair was a mess which, after all that writhing on the bed, was understandable though it enhanced the strangeness of his appearance. But it was his eyes, his great, black, unbelievable eyes that really startled him. The pupils were so dilated that they had pushed the pale grey irises to their perimeter, where they were almost invisible, just sliver-thin bands round two great balls of dark. No wonder Mrs Maling had been alarmed by his eyes. Anyone would be bound to notice though so far she was the only person of his acquaintance to see him after an LSD session. By the morning his pupils would be back to their normal size. There was nothing much he could do to improve his appearance apart from combing his hair, which he proceeded to do with a small pocket comb, and straightening his tie. An involuntary giggle irritated him. It in no way reflected how he was really feeling at that moment.

The Trip Back

When he got back to the cell he lay on the bed again. The next hour or so of waiting would be the worst but he still felt it wiser to stay as long as he could rather than risk leaving prematurely and being told to turn back. There was still a trampling of feet going on overhead and the sound of a piano playing but the party would be ending soon, at eight o'clock, and he would not be alone in the ward for long then. He thought he was progressing all right till he realised he could remember nothing between combing his hair and finding himself back on the bed. He tried recalling some detail of his return through the ward but it was all a blank: the last thing he could remember was standing in front of the mirror doing his hair. Obviously his mind had been elsewhere as he had found his way back to the cell, a condition that he must shake off before setting out for home. He could not be out on his own at night not knowing what he was doing half the time.

The piano stopped playing and soon after there was a noise of feet moving, of furniture being shifted to where it had been and a shuffling away until everything was quiet again. The Wednesday party was over for another week. A few minutes' later there was a sound of voices and movement in the ward as the dozen patients, who had been with the company above, came to bed. On none of his visits had Martin actually seen them though they had seen him, just as they were seeing him now as first one eye darkened the spy-hole, then another, till all the curious had had their fill of peeping

Feeling like some freak show Martin rolled over and pulled the blankets over his head and lay there without moving. He could still hear them talking outside the door until an imperious voice cut in and there was a clapping of hands as Mr Clement shooed them away. "Come along!" he said briskly. "Get to bed now! No hanging about, there's good lads!" The movement in the ward continued for some time, then faded away and a great weight of silence descended on the hospital like the closing of a lid. The gold coin of the spy-hole turned black as the lights in the ward went off and Mr Clement's footsteps could be heard disappearing up the ward as he returned to his dispensary den. Looking at his watch Martin saw it was quarter-past eight, another hour to go.

It was a long hour. First, he occupied it by planning the trip back: a brisk walk or run to the Wood Corner Hotel, a coin in his hand for the fare; the bus ride, his arrival at the bus station at the back of the Town Hall, which he could reach by ten, and finally the walk back to Mrs Maling's. The less he thought about her the better for the time being. At the moment he had no idea of what he was going to say to her when she saw him, red-faced, wild-eyed and giggling after he had promised her not to be coming come home looking like that again. He might even tell her the truth now that he had been taken off the LSD. It was easier to explain something when it was all over and done with than to justify something that was going to continue.

Then he switched to rehearsing what he would say to Mr Clement when the time came to try leaving.

"I'm not feeling at all bad, Mr Clement. I'd like to go home now if that's all right with you."

No, that made him sound too much like a supplicant. He must assert himself if he were to avoid staying in the hospital overnight.

"Well, I'm off now, Mr Clement. I feel perfectly all right, so there's no point in staying."

This was more like it: a simple statement of fact. After all, Mr Clement was only an employee and had no authority to forbid a patient to leave. Or had he? Martin was not sure. There was also a possibility that if one became too assertive, Mr Clement might turn awkward simply because he felt his authority was being challenged. Something more diplomatic might be called for.

"I feel all right, Mr Clement. Just thought I'd let you take a look at me before leaving."

This was neither submissive nor too assertive and would do very well, Martin thought, and he repeated the words carefully so that he could deliver them smoothly when the time came. It never occurred to him to ignore Mr Clement completely and go without asking.

At nine o'clock he got off the bed and put on his shoes, then moved about a bit, feeling fine apart from an occasional giggle. There were no gaps in his thinking as far as he could tell and his mind had been free of disturbing images for some time. When he told Mr Clement that he felt all right it would be nothing less than the truth and there was no real reason why he should not go.

The Trip Back

When it reached ten-past nine, the time for his bid to escape, Martin did up his tie, patted his hair into place, put on his raincoat and stepped outside. The ward was in darkness except at the end near the exit door where a light shone from the dispensary, and all twelve beds were rumpled with the shapes of figures under their blankets. The figure in the bed opposite the cell door stirred as Martin came out and a white face appeared suddenly above the pillow.

"Cheerio, mate!" a voice whispered. "Going home now?"

"Yes," said Martin, choked by the question and the tone in which it was asked. "Cheerio!"

The face returned under the blankets and he walked steadily up the ward towards the pool of light. If one thing were to prevent him from leaving it would be this damn giggling and he must stop himself from doing it while he was with Mr Clement. Halfway up the ward he paused and deliberately induced as much giggling as he could, rather like a swimmer taking a deep breath before going under, then pulled a straight face and stepped into the light at the dispensary door.

Mr Clement, who was sitting down reading, looked up, "Hello, there," he said. "So you're up and about then?"

"Yes," said Martin, adding with a rush, "Is it all right for me to go now?" So much for his rehearsed speeches!

"Well, you know what the doctor said," Mr Clement replied. "He wanted you to stay in. How do you feel?"

"Fine," said Martin, fixing his eyes on a green medicine bottle beyond Mr Clement's shoulder as something on which to anchor his mind.

"Let's have a look at you. You look a bit flushed to me."

Martin concentrated on the bottle label, trying to read what it said - anything to hold back the tide of giggling he could feel rising inside him.

"I think you'd better have another half-hour, don't you?" said Mr Clement after looking him over.

Martin was desperate. If he stayed there would be no bus to catch and no means of getting home, then he remembered something Mr Maling had said to him at breakfast and clutched at it as the only means he could think of to persuade Mr Clement to change his mind. Still focusing his eyes on the bottle, he said, "I particularly want to get home tonight, Mr Clement. They're broadcasting football on the telly and if I leave now I could just about get home in time to catch the end of it."

For the first time that day - or indeed any other - Mr Clement's eyes lost their wariness and they and the round face melted sympathetically.

"lucky devil'" he exclaimed, laughing. "I was hoping to see that match too. Then I got put on late duty, which spoilt everything." He paused, still smiling, and it was obvious that Martin's manoeuvre had done the trick. "All right," he said. "You can clear off, Martin, and enjoy the match. I know Wes will be watching it. I said you and he were alike."

Gripping Martin by the arm, he added, "But be careful how you go and don't forget to send in a report of today's session as soon as you can."

Elated, Martin swung away from the dispensary. "Goodnight!" he called, uttering the word just in time to prevent it from being mangled by a burst of giggling which, fortunately, Mr Clement was not close enough to hear so quickly had Martin moved up the ward. He had reached the door and already had his hand on the handle when his heart jumped. Mr Clement was calling him back.

"Just a minute, Martin!" he said.

Martin walked back, stopping a few feet from the dispensary in order that his face should not be fully in the light. How cruel if anything should happen now to prevent him from leaving! What more could Mr Clement have to say to him? Or was he just playing games with him?

When he saw Martin intended coming no nearer, Mr Clement came forward and again squeezed Martin's arm. He was one of those people for whom the act of touching seems an essential feature of their relationship with other people no matter how unwelcome it might be to the recipient.

"The doctor asked me to tell you," he said, "that as the treatment doesn't appear to be agreeing with you, there's no need for you to take the LSD again unless you want to. But he would like you to come here next Wednesday just to talk things over. If you get here about half-past three he won't keep you many minutes. All right?" This was followed by more squeezes.

"Yes," said Martin, glad that he was to be freed not only from that day's session but from any repetition of it. "It'll be a lot easier to get here after three than it has been to come early. Thanks for telling, me." He paused. "Is that all?" he asked, thinking about the time.

"Yes," said Mr Clement, releasing Martin's arm with some reluctance. "You can run along now." He laughed. "I wouldn't want you to miss your football match on television!"

Once again Martin hurried along the ward and this time got out without further hindrance. The corridor was lit with infrequent light bulbs whose wan glow gave sombre sheen to the reproduction paintings on the walls, and there was no-one about either in the passages or entrance hall, the hospital being in the grip of a silence that would not let go till morning. He saw that the hands of the hall clock were still only on twenty-past nine, indicating that he had more then enough time to get up the lane and catch the bus. He turned the brass knob on the door, half-fearing it would be locked against him, and when the door opened, was invigorated by the inrush of night air, damp and cold though it proved to be.

As the door closed behind him its thud rumbled across the tall walled brick courtyard, the innumerable windows of which were dark and sightless under their fringes of iron bars. He began to run, slowly at first, then faster as he went down the drive with its conifer trees and ponderous shadows and by the time he had reached the entrance gates he was running as fast as he could go. There was a movement by some small creature in the bushes as the gates whined open under his pressure and a mutter from the same direction as they clanged to, shutting him out in the lane. He was free!

He gave a shout and jumped so high that his outstretched hands brushed against the dome of wet branches of the overhanging trees. He was going home! Nothing could stop him now! Bouncing back to earth he grasped an imaginary partner and spun her up the lane, round and round, till the lights of the main road and the Wood Corner Hotel became too close for him to continue. If anyone had seen what he was doing and where he had come from, they would no doubt have thought that he ought to be put back inside as quickly as possible!

The hotel, so dead during the afternoon, was as bright as a lantern with light shooting out of its windows and its environs glittering with parked cars. Over the air came the twang of guitars and the beat of drum from a band entertaining the customers, smiling, chattering people strolled to and from the hotel while traffic surged along the road with its headlights flashing. The noise, the bustle, the life were a vivid contrast to the tomb-like place that Martin had just left behind.

He crossed the road to join the queue of people waiting for the bus, conscious that he was giggling occasionally and standing a little apart from the others so that they would not notice during the short time that he was there. When the double-decker bus with its number glowing on its forehead came along Martin uneasily remembered the person whom he had forgotten since going into the hospital: the angry bus conductor with the black eyebrows who had taken exception to his giggling on the return journey last week. Martin had no wish to meet him again this week or to get into a possibly violent confrontation, if the man's threats were to be taken seriously, should his giggling be observed. His eyes scanned the bus's interior till he saw with relief that the conductor was a woman with fair hair piled high on her head like a sandcastle.

"Step along there, please!" she cried as the bus stopped and the queue went aboard, "There's ample room upstairs!"

Martin went upstairs because he thought it would be more private there and it was. They were two young couples interested only in themselves and a few other people dotted about on the upper deck on their own, some apparently dozing. As the bus pulled away and began to put the miles between him and Holtwood Martin felt more relaxed. It was so dark outside that when he looked out all he could see, apart from an occasional lighted house, was his own reflection in the window, his face creasing now and then with a giggle.

He began to think about what Mr Clement had told him before he left the hospital - that he would not have to take the LSD again and that after next Wednesday's appointment, which was only going to be for a talk, he would not have to go back to Holtwood again. He would no longer have to seek Miss Cutts's help in getting away from the shop on time; he would be able to go home to Mrs Maling's at one-o'clock and after visiting Holtwood, be back home by tea-time. There would he no further need for deception. This really was going to be the last Wednesday. Things could now go back to what they were two months ago before he started the treatment.

Martin's mood changed. Was this what he really wanted - to go back to what he had been before? The whole point of the treatment had been to give him a chance to escape from that condition. What had happened to the new man he was to become? Had he now to resign himself permanently to being second-rate, a flop? There were the panics, too. Was he always to go on getting these when Mr Higlis maliciously chose to send him up to the attic? The truth was that all the deception, the visits to Holtwood, the unpleasantness of the drug, had been a waste of time. He was no better than he had been: indeed, at present he was considerably worse. He did not know yet what the eventual result of taking the drug would be or whether the fear that it had released like a genie from a bottle would go away or continue to plague him. It was easy to feel pleased now that he had been told the treatment was over and he need not continue to go to Holtwood but tomorrow, when he woke again with his limbs trembling and that voice nagging inside his head, he might feel differently.

"Enjoying yourself?"

Martin looked up to see the conductress standing over him. Her sandcastle hairdo, like her impractical high-heeled shoes, were meant to make her look taller but if anything seemed to exaggerate her shortness.

"Why?" he asked.

"Oh, I thought you must be," she laughed, "because I could see you were having a quiet chuckle to yourself. Never mind, love! The pale ale has exactly the same effect on me. What about your ticket?"

Martin gave her the fare and after receiving his ticket watched her totter along to the next customer, so his giggling was still

176

noticeable! He would have to be careful - not that anyone was likely to take much notice at this time of night when so many were either merrily going home from a pub or travelling from one pub to another and doing a fair bit of giggling themselves.

With only ten minutes of the journey to go the lights outside began to multiply as the bus entered the outskirts of the town. Inside the speed limit the lofty street lamps glared and Martin saw his reflection in the glass disappear as their glow penetrated the glass and he became more aware of what was going on around him. The bus had not got far into the town when it pulled up behind another parked bus and the conductress, who had returned downstairs, got out and started talking to a man in uniform waiting on the pavement. The other bus was empty except for its driver and was obviously about to return to the depot for the night. Martin saw the conductress give her cash satchel to the man on the pavement and walk to the empty bus, where she mounted the platform and gave the bell a pull. "Night, Bert!" Martin heard her tinny voice shout. "Thanks for waiting! See you tomorrow!" There had been a change of conductors. The woman was going off duty.

There was a scraping of metal boots as the new conductor got on board and thinking there was something familiar about the sound, Martin glanced in the mirror halfway down the stairs, saw the man's face, recognised it and panicked. It was the same man who had threatened him that afternoon - the one he had been hoping to avoid.

The man lifted his arm, the bell rang and the bus lumbered off towards the centre of the town. In the mirror, Martin saw the conductor glance upstairs, hesitate, then move off in the direction of the lower deck. "Anyone not got their tickets?" came the sound of his voice, followed soon after by the rattle of tickets being issued. The bus had got up a fair speed now. No-one seemed to be wanting to get on or off at any of the bus stops they passed and the driver was wasting no time in getting back to the bus station and the comfort of the canteen.

"Any more before I go upstairs?" came the voice of the conductor again, and at this Martin lost his nerve and knew he had to get off the bus as fast as he could. The conductress had spotted his giggling when he had been unaware of it and if this man did the same there was no knowing what he might do in view of what he had said that afternoon. It would be useless trying to explain that the giggling was unintentional: he was the sort of man who seemed to go around looking for trouble.

Martin jumped up, pressed the stopping bell regardless of what part of the town the bus was in, and stumbled to the top of the stairs as the bus rocked to a halt. It had been close to a request stop and the driver had braked sharply to pull up in time: there had been an element of mischief in his action because there had been no need to pull up quite so sharply and he must have realised, that everyone, the conductor included, would be thrown forward.

"What silly idiot pulled that bell at the last minute?" shouted the conductor as Martin scrambled down the stairs. "Some people have no bloody sense!"

Their faces met as Martin reached the platform and when the conductor saw him his reaction was as it had been that afternoon: his pale face tautened, his eyebrows hunched together in a continuous black line across his forehead and his expression bristled. "It's you again, is it?" he exclaimed. "The man with the giggle. What the hell do you think you're playing at?"

Martin intended wasting no time. The pavement was there in front of him and he made a jump for it. "I'm sorry! I didn't know the stop was so near," he shouted as soon as he had landed and felt himself reasonably safe. He could not imagine the conductor leaving the bus to come after him though from the expression on his face the man would obviously have very much liked to do so! Instead he remained on the platform giving the bell a vicious pull and as the bus moved off, waved his clenched fist and shouted, "Don't let me catch up with you again. You'll be sorry if you do!" Martin watched him standing there mouthing words till the bus had got so far down the street that it looked like a lit-up toy with a uniformed puppet gesticulating on its rear platform.

He did not worry about what had happened. All that he cared about now was that he had got away. Tomorrow he might wonder what would happen if he met the bus conductor again but for the present he was content simply to congratulate himself on his escape.

The Duck Pond Affair Etc.

At first he had no idea where he was but on looking round, recognised one or two buildings and saw that he was not far away from the railway station at the other end of the town, a good mile from home. His simplest course would have been to follow the bus down the wide well-lit main street but this would have taken him out of his way and added to the length of the journey. It would be shorter to cut through the side streets, keeping in as direct a line as possible, and this was what he decided to do. He would have to go through a part of the town that he did not often use but it had the advantage of being quiet and he was unlikely to meet anyone he knew.

He regretted his decision as soon as he had stepped out of the main road because the narrow side streets proved less well-lit with darkness draping the uneven pavements between the sporadic, inadequate street lamps. To avoid stumbling he walked down the centre of the road, there being no traffic about: indeed Martin had the streets to himself apart from an occasional cat silently slinking. The windows of the houses, mostly old decaying terraces, looked straight on to the pavement and he could see the blue glow of television screens smudging the drawn curtains and hear the tinkling of broadcast music and voices coming from inside. It was not a bad night now. The weather had cleared and he could see the stars overhead though the moon appeared to be hidden by the buildings all around.

He felt confident after walking several of the streets, some little wider than alleyways, that he was making good progress and going in the right direction: then the road in front appeared to open out as if he were entering a square, but this was an illusion. The street was no wider but there was a building with a large open space around it, a welcome gap among the tightly squeezed houses in this older, poorer part of the town. There was something familiar about this building, outlined against the night sky, and as he drew closer he recognised it as his old school, the space being caused by the playground surrounding it. One of the street lamps was close enough to the walls for him to be able to pick out the old lettering, "Infants", inscribed on a lintel of light stone above the entrance to the primary wing. The rest of the Victorian building was in red brick.

The Trip Back

It was a long time since he had been round this way but the school did not seem to have changed much. There was a small square building in the playground that had not been there in his time and that could possibly be new lavatories, he thought, and the lettering in the stone looked more worn than he remembered. What had happened to Miss Barber, his old head teacher, he wondered? Was she still at the school and did she still have her hoard of peardrops in the office with which to reward virtuous pupils and soothe unhappy ones?

This recollection gave Martin a jolt because it came back far more clearly than something should have done from so long ago. Miss Barber and her jar of peardrops were as fresh in his mind as if he had been to the school that day instead of over a dozen years ago, and then he remembered that he had been there only a few hours back while under the influence of the drug and had seen and talked to her. What was it she had said? "Oh, Martin, I am so glad to see you." We thought something must have happened to you." He had been late and she had been comforting him.

And if this were the school, then surely.... He slowly turned and looked across the road to where it began its downward slope towards the river and - yes! - there it was, not much more than fifty yards away: the corner, rising like a black cliff with the pavement winding round it on a ledge several feet above the road. It gave him a strange feeling to see it like this so soon after it had featured in his experience under the drug. It had seemed more sinister then than it did now despite the darkness and the shadows everywhere. In reality it looked just like any other street corner and nothing to be frightened of at all. As he had reached the school his journey home would follow exactly the same route, though in the reverse direction, that he had taken when he made that awful journey to the school as a child, the one that he had relived so vividly in the hospital that afternoon. He did not tempt providence by walking along the pavement, which gradually pulled away from the road, but continued down the centre of the road, thus avoiding the full impact of the corner. At the bottom of the slope he stood facing the corner's apex, where he could see both up the road towards the school and along the next road, which ended in the brightness of the main street. His short cut across the empty back streets had paid off: he would be home in far less time than if he had followed the more obvious route through the centre of the town. There was still no-one about in either direction though he could see cars flashing up and down further on.

He looked up at the corner. The pavement was several feet above him enclosed by its metal safety rail; above the pavement rose the houses, two storeys high, and above them the dim shape of roofs and chimneys disappearing into the stars. The corner was dark on one side, the same side as the school, and light on the other, where a street lamp threw its diffident glow. It was like this in his memory. He could remember clearly running towards the corner on the light side but nothing after he had turned it, on the dark.

Could anything really have happened to him here that day on the way to school? Martin did not see how it could have done. It would have been in broad daylight with houses all round and the distance was so short between there and the school. What could have happened? Yet there had been that big tear in his raincoat. How could he explain that? Well, he might have tripped as he was running or caught the coat on the safety rail or something. It was not unusual for people to damage their clothing if they were careless or in a hurry nor did it mean that they underwent an emotionally charged experience, as the doctor called it, which could fester in their mind for the rest of their lives.

Martin had doubts in any case about this theory. How could a single incident alter a person's character or change the course of his life, an incident that he could not even remember! It was rubbish! Dr Fletcher had been wrong about the LSD. He had said it would help Martin when it had done just the opposite. If the doctor had been wrong about that he could be wrong about others things too.

Turning his back on the corner, Martin walked towards the glare ahead, still keeping to the centre of the road. It was time he began thinking of what he was going to say to Mrs Maling when he got home in a few minutes' time. He had not only promised her an explanation of what he had been doing these past Wednesdays, he had also promised that he was not going to come home looking differently and here he was with his eyes still no doubt as black as coal and his face all flushed though he did not think he was giggling now. He could not recall having done this since the conductress spoke to him on the bus. What should he tell Mrs Maling? The truth? now that he could honestly say the treatment was over this might be the best thing to do, especially if he toned down the details a bit. Her horror of Holtwood might even deter her from mentioning the subject when she next wrote to his parents, who had been as much prejudiced against the place when they lived locally as everyone else was. He knew there would be a scene. She would cry and insist on depriving herself of the football match on television but no matter how much she reproached him he had that one ace to play: he could honestly say that he was never going back to Holtwood for treatment again.

By now he had reached the main road where the lofty brilliance of the street lamps banished the darkness. They stretched in a line down to the river, across the bridge and then on towards the "Royal", just distinguishable by a red splash where the cinema's neon light shone. At the junction Martin glanced up at the sign above the grocer's shop, the sign depicting the stag jumping the chasm. It had looked so fresh when he recalled it at the hospital but in the unsympathetic glare of the street lights he could see that its colour had faded and its surface was dented and rusty.

For the first time since setting eyes on it as a child, Martin no longer wanted to identify with the stag, the tautly-limbed creature leaping from one cliff's edge to the other to escape its pursuers. In all the years that he had known it, the animal had been poised like that against the sky, neither falling nor reaching the other side, just leaping in a void. What sort of existence was that? Better not to have jumped and to have been captured, better to have fallen even, than to be trapped like this, a nothing in mid-air. What use was running away if survival meant neither life nor death, only a prolongation of fear? All that Martin could feel now was pity for the stag. He would not envy it again.

A car went past and as its engine noise faded he could hear a softer sound coming from the direction of the cinema: a slap-slap on the pavement that he would not have heard had the street not gone suddenly quiet as a result of an interruption of the traffic flow.

He could see people walking away from him across the bridge on the other side of the road but the noise was not coming from them or from that last car whose red tail lights were fast drawing away in the distance. He strained his eyes in the direction of the cinema and though the street lights were bright, all that he could make out at first was a small moving blur, apparently coming towards him. It was not until it reached the bridge that he realised what it was and the sight froze him. It was a child running!

In the silvery fluorescence of the lamplights the child looked as unreal as a phantom and Martin half-doubted what he saw but as the figure started to cross the bridge he could see that it was a small boy of six or seven, the same age as himself. No, not the same age! Why had he thought such a silly thing as that? He was getting confused. It was because the drug had made him small that afternoon and now he was unsure whether it was playing tricks with him again.

It could go on having an effect long after it was supposed to have worn off. He had had that shrinking feeling days after he had been to Holtwood and bizarre images often flashed across his mind during the week between one session and another. Was it an hallucination that he was having now?

Martin looked at the group of people on the bridge to see their reaction to the running figure, if it existed, but they were certainly taking no notice of it if it did. They walked together without turning their heads towards the opposite pavement where the child was racing past at that moment. Martin felt his stomach turn and his heart begin thumping. He was imagining it all! The child was not real! His mind had slipped back into the past as it had done at the hospital and he was looking at himself making that journey to the school again. He was not in the real world at all but in some kind of hinterland where it was impossible to tell truth from fantasy. He ought not to have left the hospital.

"I don't think you ought to go home tonight," the doctor had said. He must have known something like this might happen.

Martin stood in the middle of the pavement, under the stag sign, staring at the approaching figure whose head, all white in the lamplight, bobbed up and down like a ball bouncing towards him.

The Trip Back

The child's body was swaying but its pace did not let up and when it was only a couple of lamps away, Martin, his hands clenched in his pockets, backed away and turned his head towards the wall. He did not want to see the child. He was afraid that he would be looking into his own face.

The slapping of footsteps on pavement got nearer and louder till with a sudden thump, two bodies met, the child's and Martin's, and both reeled from the collision, Martin, the heavier of the two and the first to regain his balance, saw the child stagger against the wall of the grocer's shop, gasping from the impact and the exertion of running. And it was not his own face that he saw. It was a boy he had never set eyes on before: a round-faced boy with untidy fair hair and a complexion teeming with freckles. And he was not six or seven but nearer ten though not big for his age.

"Why didn't you get out of the way?" the boy said.

"You should have looked where you were going," Martin replied, feeling bolder now that things were real again. "Why were you in such a hurry?"

The boy leaned against the wall, trying to get his breath back, his chest heaving up and down under an open-necked shirt and old pullover. "What's the time?" he said.

Martin did not bother to look at his watch. "It's gone ten," he said. "It must be several minutes past now."

The boy's mouth sagged and for a moment it looked as though he was going to give way to tears but he pulled himself together and his lips stiffened. "I've been to the pictures," he said, stepping away from the wall, "and saw the film round twice. My Mum told me I had to be back by eight. So when I get home I'm going to cop it."

After what had happened to him that day Martin felt a comradely bond with the boy, who stood there with his hands on his hips, looking braver than he no doubt felt. If there had been anything he could do, Martin would have liked to help him.

"Have you got much further to go?" he asked.

"Only as far as the school," came the reply. "We live just opposite there. I expect Mum'll be waiting for me but it won't be too bad if my Dad's there. He sticks up for me. I cant stop any longer! Must go! Cheerio!" And like a flash he had slipped past Martin into the shadows of School Road.

"Just a minute" Martin shouted.

"No!" the voice came back "I'm late enough as it is!"

Late! The word hit Martin like a slash across the face. The boy was late! He had stayed out longer than he should have done! He was going to be punished! To get to the school he would have to go round the corner! The sequence was sufficient to stir Martin into action and he followed the boy into School Road, knowing that he had to protect him though he had no idea what from.

The boy was already on the pavement on the other side of the road, running hard. Martin followed, keeping to the centre of the road, and shouted, "Stop!" though this had no effect on the boy who did not as much as turn his head. With his longer legs Martin was gaining on him but the pavement was already rising from the road and by the time he got abreast of the boy, the latter was two or three feet above him and getting higher. "Please stop!" Martin called, feeling a stab of alarm as he saw the corner in the distance but the boy kept on running though this time he deigned to answer, "Leave me alone!"

The side street was poorly-lit and the boy's fair head kept disappearing into long black pools between the infrequent lamps, like a swimmer submerging, and it was with dismay that Martin, who had slowed down when he shouted, saw the head re-appear in the glow of the next lamp. The boy had got away from him again.

The corner rose ahead: the high wall, the path, the safety rail, the drop to the road: light this side, dark the other, and Martin knew that he had to stop him from continuing, otherwise something terrible would happen. He had met the boy for the first time only a few moments ago, what happened to him was no concern of his, yet he could not bear the thought of this child running into the darkness to be caught, taken away and hung bleeding on a hook, He had to stop him!

Martin had now caught up again and the boy was directly above his head, six feet above the road. They were racing together towards the corner like a pair of riders going towards the finishing line, their joint footsteps clattering untidily in the empty street, the boy tiring now and slackening a little and falling behind and Martin slowing down, too, but for a different reason: he had just realised what had flashed across his mind. Why had he thought the boy would be hung on a hook? It was an absurd idea! Nothing like that could possibly happen to him no matter what he had done.

Why had he thought that it could? Martin knew that it must mean something and though he could think of no answer, clung to it like a rock in the flood of anxiety surging through his mind.

He could see now that he was not going to be able to stop the boy. The child took no notice when he called and Martin could not get up the wall to stop him physically because it was too high. If he had followed him along the pavement he might have been able to stop him but now it was impossible. All he could do was to watch down below while the event that he had been so anxious to prevent took place above him. The vertical line slashed upwards the boy's footsteps persisted, the body bled on the hook. Under the last street lamp the boy seemed to turn into a figure of quicksilver even his clothes shone, and he carried the light with him as he crossed the line dividing the known from the unknown, the seen from the unseen, and as Martin looked beyond the line he saw a figure emerge from the darkness, an old man wearing a dirty hat and unkempt overcoat, pushing a pram, not one of its wheels rotating in quite the same direction as the others, and cried out. Everything spun round, his legs went from underneath him and he fell to the ground. His voice cut across the night like breaking glass: a dog began barking somewhere and one or two lights went on in the windows of the houses above. The boy stopped running at last, leaned over the rail and looked down on Martin with astonishment. "What's the matter?" he shouted.

Martin was wrestling with the man, trying to get away from him, but his raincoat was caught on the pram and he could not free himself. The man was delighted. His eyes shone in the shadow cast over his upper face by the brim of his hat and his mouth, empty of teeth, opened dark and wide with a grin. "What's this then?" he said. "Are you one of them naughty boys I takes along with me?"

"No," screamed Martin. "Let me go."

"What, at half-past nine in the morning and you not at school yet?" replied the man with relish. "Oh, no! You're not a good boy! Good boys isn't late for school! Good boys get to school on time!"

His hands stretched towards Martin, their black-nailed fingers clawing at him though worn mittens.

"No!" shouted Martin. "I'm not bad, I've run all the way! Please let me go!" But the man came nearer, enjoying the power he had over the fluttering child caught on his pram. Martin could not get away. Not only was his coat caught, there was the wall of the houses on one side and the drop to the road on the other. He was trapped! His mother had been cross with him for being late and said Miss Barber, his teacher would be too. Was it they who had told the rag-and-bone man about him? Was this why he had been waiting at the corner to catch him?

When the man's fingers grabbed his shoulders, Martin gave a terrific pull, heard his raincoat tear enormously but - far more important to him at that moment - felt himself break free. He threw himself at the man, dived between his legs and once through ran off as fast as he could towards the school. From behind came the wheezing noise that was the rag-and-bone man's version of laughter and a voice cackling, "You wait! I won't forget! I'll be coming back to get you one of these days!"

Martin, who was lying on his back, opened his eyes. Above him he could see the stars. He heard someone saying, "What's the matter?" and when he raised his head, saw this fair-haired child looking down on him from the pavement above. It was the boy he had been following. "It's all right," he said. "Go on home! There's nothing to worry about," and the boy, reluctant to make himself any later, turned and ran off immediately.

No sooner had he gone than the door of one of the houses on the corner opened and against a backdrop of sudden light a man came out in his shirt sleeves and slippers and stood against the handrail almost exactly where the boy had been. "What's going on?" he said, looking down on Martin, who was still lying in the road thinking about what had happened.

Was this really his monster - the rag-and-bone man? Was he the dreadful creature with the big red mouth, body covered with scales and long tail that lay in wait for him? He knew perfectly well now that it was. He could recollect quite clearly what had happened on that morning: the gap in his journey to the school had been filled.

He had run into the corner, afraid because he was late, afraid he would be punished, and had collided with the rag-and-bone man coming the other way: the man whom children believed - were even encouraged to believe - would remove them in his pram and dispose of them to the butcher if they misbehaved. What wretched untimely luck it had been to meet him, thought Martin, at the very moment of his life when he had felt most guilty, most expectant of punishment! No wonder he had wanted to shut the experience from his mind!

Of course, the rag-and-bone man had made the most of it. He always did where small boys were concerned. He knew that later on they would torment him by calling him names, chasing him and attempting to make off with his pram, and so he tried frightening them when they were young to keep them at bay for as long as he could as means of self-protection.

"I know what's the matter with you," said the shirt-sleeved man above in a disgusted voice. "You've been drinking. You're drunk!"

Martin began to smile. Was this really his monster - the rag-and-bone man, that pathetic crippled creature with his absurd hat, trailing coat and wobbly pram fit only for the scrap heap? Was this really what he had been afraid of all these years? Was this the monster that waited for him in the dark at the foot of the attic stairs when Mr Higlis sent him up there on futile errands to demoralise him? He knew perfectly well now that it was.

Mr Higlis! Martin thought of the shop manager and started laughing, not the involuntary furtive giggling caused by the drug but spontaneous laughter that shook his body vigorously. Mr. Higlis! that huffing, puffing little bully strutting up and down the shop in his slick black coat and striped trousers! What a ridiculous figure he was! Why, thought Martin, had he not rumbled him before?

He could not stop himself from laughing. Mr Higlis was funny! Everything was funny! Mrs Maling with her quivering cheeks and bun of grey hair on the back of her head was funny! The bus conductor with eyebrows crawling across his forehead like black maggots and his voice growling like the big bad wolf's was funny! Even Holtwood was funny! Martin rolled from side to side, faced upwards to the sky, convulsed with laughter.

"If you could see yourself!" said the man above warmly. "You look disgusting! You call yourself a man? You look more like an animal rolling about like that in the gutter! People like you ought not to be allowed on the streets! You ought to be locked up! You're enough to make decent people sick!"

But Martin did not want to listen to the man. He was too busy enjoying the new world he had found where life was not something to shrink from but to be laughed at, where other people were just as frail as he was, where excuses and explanations were unnecessary, where it was less important to fit into a pattern than to create a pattern of one's own, where Wednesday - any day - was not a fearsome thing or waking up in the morning an event to be dreaded. He could not remember when he had felt so elated! The hard road on which he lay was a bed of roses!

"For two pins I'd send for the police! I've never seen such an exhibition! If this is what the drink does to you, then all I can say is the sooner you lay off it the better! To think that if a woman were to come down the street at this moment she'd have to see you like that, rolling about in the gutter! You ought to be ashamed of yourself!"

At last the voice began to rasp against Martin's mind, like the sound of a saw cutting or a fly buzzin' round a room, and looking up he saw the man to whom the voice belonged: and for all his elation, felt irritated, deeply irritated, as the voice went on rasping, sawing and buzzing. From the ends of his body he felt a sensation unlike any he had ever experienced before: it was as though his veins were filling up with hot liquor, making his body glow. The only time he could remember anything like it was at Doris's wedding when he had gulped down a glass of what he had been led to believe was lemonade but which proved to have been filled by some joker with neat whiskey.

The feeling he was getting now had the same hot, tingling sensation that the whiskey had given him. Then, as padlocked doors crashed open in his mind, he recognised this feeling for what it was: good, honest, rampant irrepressible rage! For the first time in his life he was really angry. He was not going to be spoken to like that by anyone!

Getting to his feet he stood legs apart in the road, looking up at the man who was still going on and on, and said with a voice that amazed him by its strength and confidence, "I'm not drunk, do your hear! Not drunk! And what's it to you if I am?" Then throwing back his shoulders and looking the man straight in the eye, he went on firmly, belligerently, "So shut that big mouth of yours will you! Or do you want me to come up there and shut it for you!" The man went back inside the house. Quickly.

Powick Hospital stopped admitting patients on December 5, 1978, and finally closed on March 7, 1989.